East Anglian Recipes
300 years of
housewife's choice

MARY NORWAK

Larks Press

For
Sophie, Matthew and Unity

First printed and published in England by
East Anglian Magazines Ltd. In 1978

New edition published by
The Larks Press
Ordnance Farmhouse, Guist Bottom, Dereham,
Norfolk NR20 5PF
01328 829207

November 1996
Reprinted March 2002

Printed by the Lanceni Press, Garrood Drive, Fakenham, Norfolk

Drawings by Lynn Sheridan

ISBN 0 948400 50 1

CONTENTS

Introduction   5

East Anglian Food   6

Chapter 1   Soups   8

Chapter 2   Fish   10

Chapter 3   Meat, Poultry &Game   14

Chapter 4   Sweet Puddings & Pies   23

Chapter 5   Breads, Cakes & Biscuits   30

Chapter 6   Preserves, Pickles & Home Remedies   38

Chapter 7   Wines, Syrups & Cordials   41

Chapter 8   Dumplings   45

Chapter 9   East Anglian Specialities   48

Chapter 10   Elizabeth Ravell's Book   52

Introduction

East Anglia has always been part of my life. My father's forbears were scattered over Essex and Norfolk, and the farthest west they ever seemed to reach was Bedfordshire. Although my childhood was spent on the outskirts of London, holidays were always in the eastern counties, and my adult life has been divided between the Essex/Suffolk border and Norfolk - there is no other part of the world for which I feel so great an affinity, or in which I am more at peace.

For years I have been interested in the food of the area, realising that dishes which had been served in my childhood were in fact my father's favourites, mostly from Norfolk, but when this book was proposed I was worried about finding enough material. So many regional dishes are simply handed down through families with no written record (they used to say there were far more cooks than readers in the world), and printed sources are notoriously unreliable, simply repeating and often debasing recipes which have been noted by authors who have obviously not visited the region.

My starting point was a manuscript book kept by Elizabeth Garden of Redisham in Suffolk in the years from 1847. She was a member of the gentry, and her book began life as an Eton exercise book. She had kept it as a commonplace book as many women (and men) did, recording pieces of poetry, proverbs, jokes, useful addresses, and dozens of recipes. Her family was in the interesting transitional stage from country to town living which became common as the 19th century wore on. She recorded names and addresses of good tradesmen in both London and Paris, and many of her favourites are for the sort of dishes which were retained in the nursery by Victorian servants who came from the country and have passed down to us as the favourite foods of generations of middle and upper-class men.

Although these recipes are delightful and easily used, most of them are directly descended from recipes printed in cookery books which were then widely distributed. I began to search further through printed collections of regional recipes, but few rang true to someone who lived in the area, and many were vague about origins and details.

An article in the *East Anglian Magazine* requesting local information yielded rich fruit however. Among a number of letters was one offering me a manuscript book which turned out to be mainly of the late 18th and early 19th century recipes. It had been found discarded outside a Colchester solicitor's office along with farm account books of 1754, and is full of recipes which come from families from such familiar Essex and Suffolk names as Notcutt, Quilter and Strutt. These were genuine family recipes from farmhouses and from such towns as Ipswich, Felixstowe and Colchester, owing nothing to printed books.

The final treasure arrived in the form of another manuscript book with Hadleigh and Needham Market origins, dated 1704 but with much earlier recipes which had been written in it when Elizabeth Ravell was given it. This book contains richness in the form of Elizabethan recipes and splendid herbal prescriptions, and completed a picture of East Anglian food stretching over some 300 years.

All regional recipe-seeking is a form of detective work and one intriguing clue has turned up. The earliest book stretches over more than 100 years and records a recipe from Mrs Hicks, given in 1791. The second recipe book, dating somewhere between 1754 and the end of the century, was kept by Elizabeth Hicks. Was there perhaps a time when the two books were kept in neighbouring houses or villages?

I have had correspondence from a number of people in the course of preparing this book, but my particular thanks are due for information and for the loan of manuscripts to Dorothy Hall, Ivy Halls and Elizabeth Prentice, who have made my search for authentic recipes so stimulating and exciting. I have retained the original spellings and misprints wherever the meaning is clear.

Mary Norwak

East Anglian Food

Anyone who sets out to write a history of British regional food is a brave and foolhardy person. French cuisine is carefully structured so that a named recipe is always made in the same way with identical ingredients, and regional variations are carefully noted. No kitchen regimentation for the British, however, who rely on 'a bit of this and a bit of that' according to supplies and the mood of the cook, and who scorn to write down the exact details of a favourite recipe. Even worse is the conviction that each personal or regional recipe is the only possible one, so that mild fighting can break out on the exact composition of a pork pie or the correct way to make a Yorkshire pudding. There are historical misconceptions to muddy the issue too, the main one being that England was founded on a rich diet of roast beef and plum pudding. Only a few months ago, I heard a lecturer express surprise to her audience that her grandmother's hand-written recipe book contained no beef recipes, but plenty for rabbits. It was no surprise to her middle-aged audience who hastened to tell her that as late as the middle of this century few country families saw what they called 'butcher's meat', relying instead on rabbits and pigeons, the occasional chicken, and a share-out of a neighbour's pig on rare occasions.

Local produce was obviously the guiding factor in preparing family recipes, so that in East Anglia for instance, dishes made from flour ruled supreme, with a host of recipes for fish, pigeons and hares, and the occasional luxury of a dish made from the universal cottage pig. A few turkey dishes and ways with fruit reflected changing habits in farming, while beef recipes are scarce, and East Anglian cheeses now non-existent. Defoe despised Suffolk cheese as 'the worst in England' because the quality of the milk was so poor, and Essex enjoyed a terrible reputation. The fully-flavoured sweet-cured Suffolk hams, however, made up for the cheese disaster.

East Anglia was for many hundreds of years considered a rich area by the rest of England. The land was suitable for extensive corn-growing, and for raising flocks of sheep. The cornlands and woodlands provided vast stocks of game, and the long coastline provided the best fish in the country. The growing of soft fruit and tree fruit became an important sideline. When fish was obligatory eating for religious reasons on so many days, the East Coast ports became rich and prosperous. Proximity to Europe created ports which exported wool, grain and salt fish, while the great roads from Lynn, Norwich, Ipswich and Colchester carried fish, poultry and vegetables to the ever-growing population of London.

As a result of this profitable trading, East Anglia grew rich and prosperous, with its huge houses and estates, bustling ports and towering churches. The decline of compulsory fish-days, of the wool trade and of corn-growing almost spelt disaster to the formerly prosperous area during the 19th and 20th centuries, and only now are the eastern counties beginning to prosper again.

Entry into the Common Market has stimulated a revival in the coastal ports, new industries are being founded and Europeans are buying up precious farming land. East Anglia is the land of free enterprise and many natives and newcomers are starting their own small businesses, many connected with food. There is a consequent revival of interest in such regional delicacies as crabs, smoked fish, samphire, dumplings and shortcakes, and more and more visitors come to sample local specialities. These eastern counties have a curious fascination for many who come to visit and stay to live and enjoy the wide skies, the rolling cornlands and the endless marshes, and copy again the simple lives of their ancestors who lived off local produce.

Due to the quantity of material which I have found in the course of preparing this collection of regional recipes, it has been necessary to confine the area to Norfolk, Suffolk and Essex. There are many arguments about the true boundaries of East Anglia, but all would agree that Norfolk and Suffolk form the heartland of the area. The western Fenlands fringe into Cambridgeshire, and the northern coastal regions into Lincolnshire, and one or two recipes from these areas have been included where they have some obvious connection with the main counties of East Anglia. I have included Essex, so often disregarded and treated as no-man's land, because the county has such close affinity with Norfolk and Suffolk. Today, there is a constant movement between families in the three counties, and many are closely related. Essex formed the vital link between the other two counties and London, while methods of farming and the crops produced were similar and the coastal marshes produced the same tough breed of seamen and fishermen. The same climate has produced crisp winters, howling winds and hot dry summers throughout the three counties, from which derives similar countryside so that northern Essex shades gently into Suffolk, along the valley of the Stour and the wooded uplands of the north-west, while Suffolk and Norfolk join almost imperceptibly along the Waveney valley - the three counties cannot be divided.

Bibliography

A number of minor sources have been consulted, but for those who want to know more of the background to East Anglia and the food eaten through the centuries I would particularly commend:

Tudor Food and Pastimes: F.G.Emmison (Ernest Benn Ltd.)
Bygones: (a series of books based on a TV series by Anglia Television)
The Diary of a Country Parson: James Woodforde (Oxford University Press)

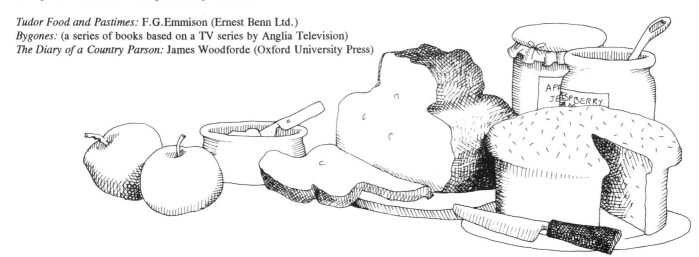

CHAPTER 1

Soups

There are few soup recipes in old manuscript books, possibly because in country districts a hearty soup would simply be made from any oddments around the house, either fresh vegetables and pieces of meat, or leftovers. Many of the soups seem to have been made from water left from boiling fish or meat and were merely a useful filler for a hungry family rather than a manifestation of the cook's art.

Westerfield White Soup (Suffolk)

1lb veal bones and pieces; 1 quart water; 1 small onion; 4 peppercorns; ½ blade mace; ¼ pint cream; Arrowroot for the thickening; 1 oz vermicelli; Salt to taste.

Wash the bones, then bring them to the boil and simmer very gently with the onion, salt, peppercorns and mace until the liquid is reduced by one third. This will take 3-4 hours. Strain the soup and set aside to cool, then skim off fat and return soup to a clean pan. Add cream and thicken with a little arrowroot mixed with a little cold milk. Boil vermicelli in salted water, drain and add to soup before serving. This recipe is dated 1876.

Suffolk Sheep's Head Broth

1 sheep's head and trotters; 2 quarts water; 2 onions; 2 carrots; 4 peppercorns; 2 turnips; 1 bunch sweet herbs; Salt to taste.

Wash well the head and trotters and put them in a saucepan with the peppercorns and sweet herbs and simmer gently for 3 hours. Strain the soup, then cut the meat from the head and mince it and the vegetables. Add to the soup and simmer for a further hour. Season well and serve very hot.

Essex Potato Soup

2 heads of celery; 1 carrot; 1 onion; 1 parsley root; and some leeks.

Boil together in some stock with a little butter. Take some floury potatoes, cook, and rub through a hair sieve. Boil with the other ingredients.

A Good Vegetable Soup (Essex)

Boil bones for 6 or 8 hours, then strain the liquor off. When cold, take all the fat completely off. Mince somewhat small a couple of turnips, a very little onion, a piece of shallot, and some outside pieces of celery. Let the stock boil for 20 minutes before it is required for dinner, then throw in the minced vegetables and a tiny bit of butter. Let the stock and vegetables boil rapidly for half an hour and, if the soup is not sufficiently thick with the vegetables, mix a teaspoonful of flour smoothly with cold water and strain it in, and let it simmer at once. Then strain it into the soup tureen, in which you can put the toast that was left from breakfast, cut into tiny squares.

Essex Green Pea Soup

Half a pint of shelled peas; 1 quart of the green shells; 1½ pints of water; 2 ounces of butter; 1 onion; 2 sprigs of mint; 2 lumps of sugar; half a pint of milk; 1 teaspoonful of cornflour.

Shell the peas, rinse the empty shells and, with a sharp knife, remove the strings. Melt the butter in a very clean saucepan, put in the peas, the prepared shells, the onion sliced, and toss (to absorb the flavour of the butter) over a slow fire for a few minutes, *but do not brown.* Then add the water, mint, sugar, and boil until tender. Rub all through a hair sieve. Blend the cornflour smoothly with the milk. Put the soup back into the saucepan, add the milk and cornflour and stir until it boils. Season and serve

Tasty Soup (Essex)

Take the liquor in which codfish has been boiled, and add to each quart half a teacupful of tapioca, a carrot, half a head of celery, and a little parsley. Cut the vegetables up very small and boil until they are cooked. Then thicken with flour. Add pepper and salt to taste, and serve with dry toast cut into small fancy shapes. This is very tasty and, costs very little.

Miss Buchanan's Ipswich Partridge Soup

Take a brace or a leash of partridges dressed the day before. Beat them in a marble mortar, bones and all and be careful that all the bones are broken, then take a quart or three pints (according to the quantity of soup you wish to make) of good beef broth and put it in a saucepan with the pounded partridges and 6 onions with 2 cloves stuck in each and a carrot. Stew them all together very slowly for 3 or 4 hours, or till the juices are all extracted, and if you have any cold ham in the house add a slice or two of the lean. When stewed, strain it through a sieve and press as much of the liquor out as you can do with the back of a spoon. Then take a piece of butter about 2 or 3 ozs and work as much flour into it as you can (at least a tea-cup full) with your hands a little at a time. Then break it in smallish pieces and put it in a basin and take 2 or 3 spoonfuls of the soup when quite hot and put to it. Stir it about till it is mixed and like a thick cream, then put it to the soup and boil it all together, stirring it frequently. Before you send it to table add ¼ pint of cream and a little cayenne pepper, but do not let it boil after the cream is in, as it will curdle. It should be about the thickness of pease soup. Hare soup may be made exactly the same with the remains of a hare that has been dressed. *Mrs Garden 1847*

Essex Pea Soup

4 pints of water; 1 pint of dried peas; 3 onions; 3 carrots, 2 turnips, a bunch of herbs; sixpennyworth of beef bones (or stock from boiling salt beef).

Soak the peas in two or three waters for 12 hours, wash the bones, put them in a clean saucepan with the water and peas, add salt and pepper, skim well while boiling. Scrape the carrots, peel the turnips, skin the onions, cut them all in dice, add to the bones and peas, simmer very gently for 4 hours. Remove the bones, season with dried mint if liked, rub through a hair sieve if a purée is required. The water in which a joint of salt beef has been boiled , or one pint of bone or vegetable stock can be used instead of the bones.

Essex Milk Soup

Take 4 large potatoes and 1 onion, peel and cut them into quarters, and put them into 2 quarts of boiling water or white stock. Boil till done to a mash, strain through a colander and rub the vegetables through with a wooden spoon, return the pulp and soup to the saucepan, with one pint of milk, and bring to the boil; when it boils, sprinkle in 3 tablespoonsful of crushed tapioca, stirring all the time. Boil 15 minutes, and serve.

CHAPTER 2

Fish

East Anglia is famous for the variety and quality of its fish. Foremost is the herring which made Yarmouth great in the days when the eating of fish was compulsory on many days for religious reasons. Yarmouth and Lowestoft sold tons of fresh herrings, salted or pickled herrings and the heavily smoked red herrings. Kippers were prepared from herrings gutted before smoking, but bloaters were lightly salted herring smoked without gutting, so that the gut imparted a gamey flavour. The Great Yarmouth Herring Fair, which lasted for 40 days, was first held in 1270 and went on until well into the 18th century. During the 19th and early 20th century, Scots women came down from Banffshire in November for the herring gutting and packing.

All along the East Anglian coast, delicious fish have provided work for thousands and supported villages and towns. At Leigh, near Southend in Essex, there is almost a miniature village of sheds where the boiling of cockles, winkles and shrimps is carried out. At Colchester, there are the famous oyster beds founded by the Romans in which English native oysters are bred. At Orford in Suffolk and Morston in Norfolk, other types of oysters are laid to fatten and can be eaten all the year round (English native oysters spawn during the summer and are therefore protected during the breeding season which occurs 'when there is no R in the month' when they could traditionally not be eaten).

Cromer is famous for its crabs, Sheringham for lobsters, Southwold for soles, Wells for whelks and Kings Lynn for shrimps, while mackerel, mussels and cockles appear in their due season. Dabs or flounders are another popular catch outside estuaries on the sandy shore bottom; these little flat fish are delicious lightly floured and shallow-fried in butter.

Cockles

The best cockles are said to come from Stiffkey, near Wells, and are known as 'Stewkey Blues' because they have a dark grey-blue shell. They are meaty little chaps and richly tasty. It is best to clean cockles by putting them into fresh water with a little porridge oats so that they open to take in the 'food' and get rid of any sand. When they have cleaned themselves after an hour or two, cockles should be washed and put into a heavy pan without further moisture. Put the lid on and heat gently and they will quickly open and be ready to eat. The nicest way is in their shells in their own liquor, with a libation of hot melted butter. They can be left to cool in their liquor and then served cold with salt, pepper and vinegar, but the flavour is not so delicate this way.

Shrimps

Pink shrimps and small brown shrimps are commonly available, and the tiny brown ones are reputed to have the sweetest flavour although they are so troublesome to peel. If shrimps are cooked in fresh water instead of salt water, they are easier to peel. Of course they are delicious served cold with thin brown bread and butter, but peeled shrimps are also very special if reheated gently in a little butter with a pinch of nutmeg and black pepper.

Herring Pies

For many years, the city of Norwich had to deliver 24 herring pies each year to Court. This feudal tenure originated before the foundation of Yarmouth when the valley of the Yare was still an estuary, and Norwich was an important fishing station. The city sheriffs made annual provision for the manufacture of these pies which were sent to the Lord of the Manor of Carleton, to be carried by him or his tenant to the royal palace and placed on the sovereign's table.

In 1673, 100 of the first new herrings in the city were delivered which were made into 24 pies, well seasoned with half a pound of ginger, half a pound of pepper, a quarter of cinnamon, 1 ounce of spice of cloves, 1 ounce of long pepper, 'halfe an ounce of grains of paradise and halfe an ounce of galangals'. These were delivered to Charles II by Edward Eden, who received in return 'six loves, six dishes out of ye kitchen, one flaggon of wine, one flaggon of beer, one truss of hay, one bushel of oats, one prickett of wax, and six candles of tallow'.

The Norwich herring pies were obviously carefully inspected by the household officers to the court. In 1629, there was a complaint from Hampton Court that the pies 'were not well baked in good strong pastye as they ought to have been', some only contained four herrings instead of the statutory five, and they were not made of the *first* new herrings which reached the city.

Southend Whitebait

Whitebait are best eaten during the period from March to August. Wash and dry the fish, toss lightly in flour and fry in deep fat. Drain and when all are done, return to the basket and fry in very hot fat until crisp. Sprinkle with salt and serve with lemon and brown bread and butter. This double-frying is the secret of good whitebait cooking.

Eel Pie

Clean, skin and cut 1¾ eels into pieces 2 inches long. Dry each piece separately, placing a piece of butter inside, with a little pepper, salt and chopped parsley. Lie them in a pie dish with a cupful of vinegar and water mixed. Thicken with a teaspoon plain flour (or cornflour). Cover with a good puff pastry, and bake in a hot oven. Serve cold for Sunday tea.
**Eels were a great favourite in Norfolk and caught by means of special traps.*

Plump Whiting

A number of moderate-size whiting are cleaned and washed, laid in salt for a few hours (more or less according to taste) and afterwards hung up in the sun for about 2 days, not longer. When wanted for use, boil them lightly on a very clear fire, and serve very hot. The middle-sized are the best for table; the smaller ones bony and the very large of too great a size to fry.
Mrs.Garden 1847

Suffolk Perch

Perch; Chopped tomatoes; Chopped onions; Thyme; Oil; Home or farm cider; Soft roes; Brown breadcrumbs; Chopped parsley.

Put the oil into a lidded casserole, then add the chopped tomatoes and onions, salt and pepper, and thyme, and soften over low heat. Make a stuffing with the soft roes, a little onion and just a trace of tomato; bind with the breadcrumbs, season and stuff the fish. Half bury the fish in the chopped vegetables, add the cider, and sprinkle the top of the fish with oil. Cook in the oven with the lid on. Sprinkle with parsley and serve. Diced potatoes can be added to the chopped vegetables if you wish.

**This is an old recipe which makes the best of perch, and it is very good made with Aspall cyder. Cook the dish in a moderate oven (350°F, 180°C, Gas Mark 4) for 40 minutes.

Mrs Dowson's Stewed Eels

1 teaspoon black pepper; 2 teaspoons salt; ½ an onion; chopped parsley.

Simmer eels in 1 pint of milk for ¼ of an hour. Braid a piece of butter in some flour and add to it about 5 minutes before it is served up. A little lemon juice to be added. The eels are not to be put into water and not skinned - to be wiped with a cloth.

Mrs.Garden 1847

Suffolk Trout

4 river trout; 4 bay leaves; 2 oz butter; Juice of 1 lemon.

Clean the trout and remove their heads. Put a bay leaf inside each trout. Melt the butter in a thick frying pan and put in the trout. Add the lemon juice and cover with a lid. Cook on a very low heat for 20 minutes, turning the trout once during cooking. Serve very hot with lemon slices, peas and new potatoes.

Suffolk Shrimp Pie (1823)

Pick a quart of shrimps. If they be very salt, season them only with mace and a clove or two. Bone and mince 2 or 3 anchovies, mix them with the spice and then season the shrimps. Put some butter at the bottom of a shallow pie dish. Put in the shrimps and pour over them some more butter and a glass of sharp white wine. Cover with a very thin delicate piecrust and bake until this is cooked. It won't take long.

Pickled Salmon (Essex)

Boil the salmon in salted water, with 2 lumps of sugar and 1 gill of vinegar in it. Let it simmer until done. Then take it out and put into vinegar that has been well spiced with mixed pickling spice and a small piece of ginger. The vinegar must cover the fish. You can keep it thus until required.

Pickled Mackerel (Essex)

Six smallish mackerel; 4 bay leaves; 4 cloves; 1 level teaspoonful of peppercorns; 1 pint vinegar; thyme; parsley; fennel (if possible), salt and pepper.

Fillet the mackerel, wash and dry them, stew over them the herbs finely minced, and a little pepper and salt. Put in a dish with a little butter, and bake till cooked. Try with a skewer and see if they are done. Boil the vinegar, bay leaves, cloves, and peppercorns together for ten minutes. Stir in a teaspoonful of extract of meat, and when cold, strain the liquor over the fish. Let it stand for several hours before serving, then drain, put on a clean dish, and garnish with parsley.

To bake Mackerel

Open them and take out the roes. Wash them and cut off the heads and tails. Wipe them dry and take out the bones, and season them with pepper, salt, mace and nutmeg mixed. Lay them as close as you can in a long pan and cover them with red wine and good vinegar of each an equal quantity. Cover the pan with paste and bake in a slow oven.

Mrs Garden 1847

Aldeburgh Sprats

Sprats may be smoked, dried, potted or fried; but being very oily, they are best broiled. They are in season in November and during the winter. To broil sprats, clean them well, dry them and roll or toss lightly in flour. Broil on a closely barred gridiron over a clear fire or under the gas griller. Turn them in about 3 minutes. If preferred, they may be cooked in a hot dry frying pan, as there is sufficient oil in the fish to prevent them sticking or burning. As with whitebait, their flavour is improved by the addition of a little lemon juice and cayenne pepper. The first catch of the season used to be sent to London for the Lord Mayor's Banquet.

Yarmouth Red Herrings (1823)

Choose those that are large and moist. Cut them open and pour over them some boiling small beer. Let them soak half an hour, then drain and dry them. Make them just hot through before the fire, and rub them over with cold butter. Serve with egg sauce or buttered eggs; mashed potatoes should also be sent up with them.

Herring and Potatoes (Essex)

Wash, and boil some potatoes carefully, so that they do not break or get too soft. Drain them, peel, and slice them rather thickly. Keep them hot. Fry lightly a chopped onion in 1 ounce of butter. Dust in some flour, and 3 tablespoonfuls of vinegar, salt and pepper, and a bay-leaf, and not quite a pint of water. Put the pan to simmer at the side of the stove. Take 2 red herrings, wash them well, cut them lengthways, and remove the bones. Cut up the flesh small, and let it simmer in the sauce for a few minutes. Put in the potatoes next, stirring carefully so as not to break them. Then add 2 ounces of butter and 1 gill of milk, and stir all well over the fire till it reaches boiling point.

Bloater Paste

Grill or bake 3 fat bloaters until the skin is crisp (use a moderate oven or grill for this). Skin and bone them and weigh the flaked flesh. Take the same weight of butter and mash the fish and butter together, adding a pinch of Cayenne pepper. Bloaters may also be cooked in hot water, to avoid cooking smells, but they are not so good this way. Bloater paste used to be served at breakfast, but is now more acceptable with toast for tea. It should be pressed into small china pots for service.

Norfolk Sea Pie

1 lb cod fillet; ½ pint medium sweet cider; 1 lb cooked potatoes; Salt and pepper; A little milk; 1 oz butter; 1 oz plain flour; 2 tomatoes; 2 oz grated cheese.

Cut the cod in cubes and put into a pan with the cider. Cover and simmer for 20 minutes. Drain the fish and keep the cooking liquid. Put the fish into a pie dish, piling it in the centre. Mash the potatoes well with salt, pepper and milk, and arrange round the fish. Melt butter, stir in the flour and cook for 1 minute. Gradually add the fish liquid and bring to the boil, stirring well. Season with salt and pepper and pour over the fish. Slice the tomatoes and arrange on the top, then sprinkle it with grated cheese. Brown under the grill or at the top of a hot oven, and serve at once.

CHAPTER 3

Meat, Poultry and Game

Few country people saw 'butcher's meat' and it is a myth to think they lived on huge spit-roast joints of beef and lamb. The pig reigned supreme, producing valuable fresh meat, meat for salting, delicious offal, and quantities of pies and brawn. Solid pudding crusts eked out oddments of meat, either in the form of a pudding or roly-poly, or were cooked under the meat to be served first to lessen the appetite (dumplings were served for the same reason.

Chickens and ducks were used sometimes, but much of the family's meat came from rabbits, hares and pigeons. In the rich corn-growing land of East Anglia, game of all kinds was plentiful, and the partridge of the eastern counties has always been famous.

The Cottage Pig

Every cottage family used to keep a pig, 'the gentleman who pays the rent', and pork was the only carcass meat many country families knew until after the Second World War. Meat was normally provided by hares, rabbits and game birds, and perhaps the poultry which scratched around the house. Country people never saw what they called 'butcher's meat' but relied on swopping pieces of pork with the neighbours; and pig-killing was an important event. The smallest pig of a litter was often called the 'peppermint' and would be cosseted by the children until it grew sturdy.

Nothing was ever wasted from the pig. They used to say you could use everything but the squeak. Fat was rendered down into lard, flavoured with rosemary, and commonly eaten instead of butter on bread by the children. The most perishable parts of the pig were used first. The chitterlings or runners (intestines) could be boiled to eat hot or cold, or might be cut up and baked with apples and currants between two pastry crusts (chitterlings are difficult to find these days, but are often available at Yarmouth market). Fat was used to cover the pig's fry (see recipe) which might be served with Norfolk dumplings. Odd pieces of pork were made into sausages and pork cheese, while joints were salted or distributed among neighbours.

Pig's Fry

The fry consists of pig's kidney, liver, heart and melt, with some pork belly added, and is particularly popular in Norfolk and Lincolnshire. The fry can be simply sliced and fried, but older people cut it up and put it in a tin with sliced onions, salt and pepper and a little pork dripping or pieces of pork fat. Some sage can be added too, and the fry is baked in a moderate oven for about an hour and a half. The cooking liquid can be thickened for gravy, and the resulting dish is very tasty.

Faggots or Savoury Ducks

These were made from pig's fry complete with the thin fat skin known as 'veiling', 'kell' or 'caul'. The Lincolnshire version is made into one large loaf shape known as Haslet.

Make the faggots from 1 lb fresh breadcrumbs and 1 lb pigs fry with sage, salt and pepper. Cut up the fry into small pieces with 4 oz chopped onions, cover with cold water and bring to simmering point very slowly. Take off the heat and leave to cool then mince and add to enough breadcrumbs to make a soft consistency which is not too wet. Season and mix thoroughly. Shape the mixture into large round balls and cover each one with a piece of caul. Put into a greased tin and cook at 350°F, 180°C, Gas Mark 4 for 45 minutes. Serve with gravy made from any pan juices and the liquid in which the fry was cooked. Serve hot with creamy mashed potatoes. Haslet which is made in a similar way can be served cold.

Fritter Pie

Surplus pig fat was cut into small pieces and cooked very gently over low heat or in a very low oven until the fat ran. This fat should be poured off at intervals until it ceases to run. This gives a good lard which can be used for cooking. The remaining crisp pieces of pork are known as 'fritters' or 'scratchings' and used to be mixed with apples, brown sugar, sultanas and spice as a filling for a two-crust plate pie. The 'fritters' also used to be added to fruit cake mixtures.

Bacon

Bacon was prepared from the sides and smoked in the farmhouse or cottage, or could be taken to the local 'smokey house', often owned by a local craftsman, who could use up his sawdust, oak chips and wood shavings. The sawdust was dampened down to make it smoke and the bacon and ham might take three weeks to be smoked. Traditionally Suffolk hams were sweet-cured with black treacle, brown sugar and hot beer. The almost black Bradenham ham can still be found at Harrods in London.

Hams were cooked in the kitchen copper with a bunch of hay in the bottom to stop them sticking; and this imparted a special flavour - a ham was a great treat at Christmas, or one of the great farming occasions such as sheep-shearing or harvest-time. Brick bread ovens were sometimes used to bake hams in a thick layer of dough or 'huff paste' which kept the meat moist. The juice-soaked crust was sometimes eaten by servants, or might be put into the hen bucket.

Epping Sausages

6 pounds of young pork, quite free from skin, gristle or fat. Cut it small and beat it fine in a mortar. Chop 6 pounds beef suet very fine, with a handful of sage leaves. Spread the meat on a clean dresser, and shake the sage over it. Shred the rind of a lemon fine, and throw it with sweet herbs on the meat, 2 nutmegs grated, a spoonful of pepper, with a large spoonful of salt. Throw the suet over, and mix all well together. Put it down close in a pot and, when it is to be used, roll it up with as much egg as will make it smooth.

Suffolk Sweet Cured Ham

Rub the pork with cooking salt and a little saltpetre (this gives a pink colour to the ham, but too much will make it hard - usually about 2 oz to 2 lb salt will be the right proportion) and put into an earthenware crock glazed on the inside. Cover and leave for a week, rubbing in the salt mixture each day. Wipe the ham. Wash out the pot and dry it. Put in 2 lb black treacle, 2 lb soft brown sugar and 2 pints hot stout. Put in the ham and rub well with the mixture. Weigh down the meat so it remains under the pickle and leave a large ham for about 6 weeks, although smaller pieces of meat will be ready sooner. The ham should be hung in a cool airy place away from flies for about 4 days before being smoked.

Norfolk Pork Cheese

1 salt pork hock with trotter, Pepper, powdered sage.

Simmer in water to cover for about 1½ hours, until the meat falls off the bones. Cut the meat into pieces and toss them lightly in pepper and sage. Put the bones back in the liquid and boil them until the stock is reduced to half a pint. Strain over the meat, mix well and pour into bowls. When cold and beginning to set like a jelly, mix again and pack into smaller bowls. Cover and place light weights on top until fully set.

Essex Brawn

Procure a pig's head which has been in salt not more than 3 or 4 days. Wash it and put it on in sufficient water to cover it well. Let it cook gently for about 3 hours, until quite tender, then take it out, remove the bones (which should come away easily) and cut up all the meat in small pieces, putting it into a basin, which should be kept hot over boiling water, or the brawn will set too soon. Season with pepper (no salt) and a little powdered mace and sage if liked; put into a pressing tin if one is at hand, and pour over the meat about half a pint of the liquor in which it has boiled. If a brawn tin is not to be had, use an ordinary large cake tin, put a plate closely fitting on top, and set on that the heaviest weights you have - either scale-weights or irons.

Suffolk Sausages

6 lb pork sausage meat, 2 oz salt, Pinch of mace, Pinch of cloves, ¼ oz pepper, Pinch of nutmeg, 5 oz soft breadcrumbs, ¼ pint hot water, Sausage skins.

Mix all ingredients well and put into skins. Boil these sausages before frying them.

Essex Brain Cakes

Well wash and clean the brains, then put them into a pan of boiling salted water slightly acidulated with lemon juice, and let them cook over a slow fire for an hour; lift them out, drain well and leave until cold; then cut into rounds, egg and breadcrumb them, and fry in hot fat.

Suffolk Sweet Cured Bacon

Take 1 quart of beer, 1 lb granulated sugar, 1 lb bay salt, ½ oz peppercorns, 1 quart best vinegar, ½ oz saltpetre, 1 lb cooking salt, ½ oz cloves. Boil all together. Take 2 oz hops and boil in a quart of water for half an hour, strain and add to liquid already obtained from the above ingredients. Pour over meat when cold. This is a very good method of curing hams and bacon.

Essex Devilled Cutlets

1½ lb of nicely trimmed cutlets, 2 oz of butter, quarter of a pint of cream, 1 teaspoonful of cornflour, 1 small teaspoonful of mustard, a good pinch of cayenne, 2 dessertspoonfuls of Worcester sauce.

Melt the butter in a frying pan, lay in the cutlets which should be smartly trimmed, and fry lightly till cooked. Take up the cutlets on a plate and keep hot. Put the cornflour, mustard, and cayenne into a basin, mix in the Worcester sauce gradually until smooth. Put the frying pan on the fire again with the butter still in it in which the cutlets were fried. Add the cream and stir well together. Let it boil up; now put in the Worcester sauce mixture. Stir well until it boils up and is quite smooth. Lay in the cutlets and let them stand at the side of the fire for 2 or 3 minutes until very hot through. Dish in 2 rows and pour the sauce over. If it be too thick before dishing, half a cup of milk with a small scrap of butter may be stirred in to thin it.

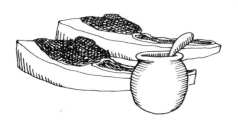

Suffolk Oxtail Brawn

1 oxtail, 1 oz butter, 1 onion, 3 cloves, Bunch of mixed herbs, Salt and pepper, 2 tablespoons vinegar, 1 hard-boiled egg.

Wash the oxtail and cut it into joints. Dry it well and dust it lightly with a little flour. Melt the butter and fry the oxtail, turning it so that it is brown all over. Add the onion stuck with the cloves, the bunch of herbs, salt and pepper and the vinegar, and cover with cold water. Bring to the boil and simmer for 4 hours until the meat leaves the bones. Cool slightly and then chop the meat. Grease a mould lightly with butter and decorate it with slices of egg. Put the meat into this mould. Return the oxtail bones to the saucepan and boil rapidly until the liquid is reduced to half a pint. Cool slightly and then fill the mould. Turn out when cold.

Essex Ham Cake

Mince finely 1½ pounds of cooked ham; boil a slice of bread in half a pint of milk, and mix this with the ham, beating them well together and binding them with a well-beaten egg. Have ready a wetted mould, pack the mixture into this, and bake for an hour in a very hot oven, by which time it should be nicely coloured; then turn out, and serve either hot or cold. Rabbit or veal may be used in the same way. Ongar Ham Cake is made in the same way, using ale instead of the milk.

Essex Hot-pot

This should be made in a round deep pie-dish.   Take 2 lb of mutton chops, 4 sheep's kidneys, and 1 lb or more of peeled potatoes. Place alternate layers of the sliced potatoes, chops and kidneys, with sliced onions, pepper and salt, till the dish is full. If liked, oysters and anchovies may be added, and are a great improvement to the flavour of the hot-pot. Cover the top of the dish with whole potatoes, and pour over it a little water for gravy. Bake in a moderate oven for full 3 hours, and let the potatoes on top be nicely browned. Fasten a serviette round the dish and serve very hot.

Norfolk Lamb in a Crust

Use a leg of lamb or mutton, wipe it and sprinkle with salt. Make up a suet crust using half as much suet as self-raising flour, or plain flour with baking powder. Wrap the leg in the crust, tie in a floured cloth and simmer in a pan of water for 4 hours. Drain and take off the crust for serving, but eat the crust as an accompaniment with gravy.

Pot Day

Until the middle of the 19th century, it was the custom amongst even very substantial farmers to cook only three times a week, of which Sunday was always one. These days of periodical cookery were called 'pot days', and as friends usually knew which days were peculiar to a family, if they intended to go uninvited to a house, they would contrive to visit on a pot day.

Hollow Meat

There were many warrens in Norfolk and the country was over-run with rabbits before the improvement of agriculture. In the light-land farms, these formed a considerable part of the diet of farming servants and were known as 'hollow meat'. It was the practice when a servant let himself to a farm to make a proviso that he should be fed 'hollow meat' only a certain number of days a week.

Suffolk Broiled Partridge

Take 2 or 3 partridges, split in halves. Sprinkle lightly with flour, salt and cayenne pepper, and broil them over a clear fire, the cut side first. Brush over with some hot butter when dished and serve with sauce. To make the sauce, melt 2 oz butter in a stew-pan, stir in 1 oz flour, cayenne and salt, and cook for 2 minutes. Then gradually add ½ pint of brown stock, let it boil up well, add 2 large tablespoonfuls of mushroom ketchup. Strain into a sauce boat.

Potato Case Pie

2 lb cooked and mashed potato; 2 cupfuls minced ham or bacon; 1 teacupful flour; 1 small onion; 1 teaspoonful minced parsley and thyme; 2 oz butter; Pepper and salt and nutmeg.

Mash the potatoes smoothly with butter, season. Work the flour into the potatoes to make a paste. Grease a cake-tin, line with some of the potato mixture, put in the minced ham with seasoning, herbs, and onion cut small. Put the potato pastry on top and bake in a quick oven for ½ an hour. Serve with brown gravy. While in mid-Suffolk, ham or bacon is used as a filling for this pie, I found that on the coast, fish, especially cooked haddock or flounders, was used, and the onion was omitted.

Mrs Arthur Webb

Suffolk Pork Cake

1 lb cooked pork; 3 small onions; 1 large apple; 2 tablespoonfuls sugar; Pepper and salt; Pastry.

After parboiling, chop the onions small. Divide the pork into little bits, peel and core and slice apple thinly. Grease an oblong shallow baking-tin, line with rough puff-paste. Spread over the pork, onion and lastly a layer of apple, season liberally with pepper and salt, scatter over 1 teaspoonful of sugar, wet edges of pastry, cover with thin pastry top. Mark with a knife into 3-inch squares. Bake in a good oven for ¾ of an hour. Serve hot or cold.

Mrs Arthur Webb

Roast Rabbit

Clean the rabbit and leave it whole in cold salted water for 2 hours. Dry and fill with stuffing. Make this with 2 onions boiled until nearly tender and chopped, mixed with breadcrumbs, salt, pepper and chopped sage. Stitch up the rabbit, sprinkle with seasoned flour and put into a roasting tin with some pieces of dripping on top. Pour in some milk to come halfway up the rabbit and cook in a moderate oven until browned, basting well with the milk which will form a gravy. Serve with potatoes and a green vegetable.

Norfolk Mussel Pudding

8 oz self-raising flour; 3 oz shredded suet; Pinch of salt; 2 pints mussels; Salt and pepper.

Make the suet crust with flour, suet, salt and water, and roll out. Put on to a piece of greased greaseproof paper. Wash the mussels well and remove their beards. Put them in a pan on a very low heat and they will open quickly. Put them on to the dough, season with salt and pepper. Tie up in a cloth and steam for 1½ hours.

Essex Pork Plugga

Make like Norfolk Mussel Pudding, using diced streaky pork instead of mussels.

Essex Rabbit Pie

In one Essex family about 50 years ago, rabbit pie was served regularly for Monday morning breakfast. During the month of May (and May only) the pies contained a mixture of rook and rabbit. At other times, the mixture could be moorhen and rabbit.

Pigeon Pudding (1)

8 oz self raising flour; 4 oz suet; 2 pigeons; 8 oz shin beef; 1 kidney.

Make up suet pastry and line a pudding basin. Cut pigeons in quarters and put in basin with diced beef and kidney. Season well and cover with stock. Put on pastry lid and steam for 2½ hours.

Pigeon Pudding (2)

8 oz self-raising flour; ½ teaspoon salt; 4 oz shredded suet; 3 pigeons; 8 oz chuck steak; 3 hard-boiled eggs; Salt, pepper and mace.

Make a suet pastry by mixing flour, salt, suet and ¼ pint cold water. Line a pudding basin with pastry, leaving enough for a lid. In the basin put the breasts of the pigeons, the steak cut in small pieces, the egg yolks, salt, pepper, and a pinch of mace. Pour in stock from the bones and trimmings, to just cover the meat. Cover with suet crust, tie on a pudding cloth, and cook in a saucepan of boiling water for 3 hours.

Norfolk Plough Pudding

8 oz self-raising flour; 4 oz shredded suet; 1 lb pork sausage meat; 4 oz bacon; 1 large onion; 2 teaspoons chopped sage; ½ oz Demerara sugar; Fresh tomato sauce.

Mix together the flour and suet with a pinch of salt and enough cold water to make a firm dough. Roll out the dough, and use two-thirds to line a 2-pint pudding basin. Press the sausage meat into the pastry all round the basin. Chop the bacon and onion and mix together with the sage and sugar. Put this mixture into the centre of the pudding and cover with the remaining pastry. Cover with greaseproof paper and a piece of foil or a pudding cloth. Steam for 4 hours, and serve with a hot tomato sauce.

Norfolk Beef Pudding

8 oz self-raising flour; 3 oz shredded suet; Pinch salt; 12 oz stewing steak; 1 shallot; Salt and pepper.

Make up a suet crust with flour, suet, salt and water. Roll it out and put on to a piece of greased greaseproof paper. Cut up the meat and shallot finely and put on to the suet pastry. Sprinkle with water and season with salt and pepper. Tie up in a cloth and steam for 3½ hours.

Suffolk Layer Pudding

6 oz self-raising flour; 6 oz plain flour; ¼ teaspoon salt; 4 oz suet; 1 lb cooked minced meat; 1 medium onion; Salt and pepper.

Mix suet pastry with 2 kinds of flour, salt, suet and milk to moisten. Line a pudding basin with half the mixture. Use meat left from the joint, or fresh mince which has been cooked, and use a little stock or gravy to moisten. Mix meat with chopped onion and seasoning. Put a layer of meat mixture into basin, then a thin layer of suet pastry, then more meat and pastry until basin is full, ending with pastry layer. Cover and steam for 2 hours. Serve with gravy or parsley sauce.

Roast Partridge

Cover the breast with bacon and roast in a moderately hot oven (375°F, 190°C, Gas Mark 5) for about 30 minutes, basting well with butter. Stir a little port into the pan juice to make the gravy, and serve half a bird to each person with watercress and game chips. Cold partridge is good for breakfast, or makes an excellent supper with salad, followed by cheese and plum cake.

Suffolk Onion Pudding

4 oz plain flour; 2 oz suet; 8 oz onions; salt and pepper.

Mix flour and suet with water to a stiff dough - and roll out. Cut up onions, salt and pepper them, and put on to dough. Roll up into a cloth. Boil for 1¼ hours. Serve with a slice of butter. This is very good with boiled bacon or a piece of beef.

Dereham Duck

6 large onions; 2 lb apples; 1 level table-spoonful chopped sage and parsley mixed; 1 cupful breadcrumbs; 1 tablespoonful sugar; Salt and pepper.

Peel the onions. Boil until nearly cooked, drain thoroughly. Carefully place on a plate and remove the centre from each. Have ready mixed the breadcrumbs and parsley and sage liberally seasoned with pepper and salt. Stuff the onions and add small knobs of dripping. Lift the stuffed onions into a hot, deep pie-dish in which dripping has been melted, baste each one, then put in the apples, peeled, cored and sliced, and the chopped centres of the onions. Season, add 2 tablespoonfuls of sugar, cover with another pie-dish, bake for ½ an hour. It was said in Norfolk that roast duck was once the poor man's dish, so general were the flocks of ducks and so commonly were they used. One farm has this substitute dish. *Mrs Arthur Webb.*

Halstead Pheasant

1 plump pheasant; 3 rashers bacon; 3 table-spoons butter; 8 shallots; Salt and pepper; 1 tablespoon brandy; 8 fl. oz veal or chicken stock; 5 fl. oz cream; 1 tablespoon grated horseradish.

Truss the pheasant and cover the breast with bacon. Brown in a casserole with butter, shallots and a little seasoning. When the bird is golden, pour in the brandy and light it (it's easier to heat the brandy gently first). Add the stock and cook for 30 minutes, basting often with the juice. Remove from the heat and stir in the cream and horseradish. Simmer for 20 minutes, basting with the sauce. Add more seasoning if necessary, then carve the bird and pour over the sauce. I find this is best cooked in a cast-iron casserole on top of the stove, as it needs frequent basting. ***This recipe came from R. A. Butler's cook at Halstead, when he was M. P. for Saffron Walden; it makes a delicious change from a plainly roasted bird.**

Forc'd Meat Balls

Cut some Veal and as much suet Season'd with Pepper, Salt and Nutmeg, some Lemmon Peel and shred Sweet herb. Beat them in a mortar together, then put in 1 egg and a little flour. Make them up and either stew or fry them with what you please. *Elizabeth Hicks: late 18th century*

In Norfolk there is a book recording the 'swan marks' of the peerage and gentry and the Public Record Office has records of marks from other countries. These were intricate patterns made on the beaks of the birds to indicate ownership. Swan was certainly eaten from the middle of the 15th century, and always formed part of the feasting in great houses, or for special events. As late as 1931, the Master, Great Hospital, Norwich, was offering cygnets (young swans) dressed for dinner and banquets, or alive for ornamental waters, through an advertisement in *The Times*. The great cook Francatelli gave a recipe in the 1850's for a Norwich-fed cygnet, so it would seem these were certainly superior birds. Cygnets were usually used, and in best condition in September. They were often cooked in the same way as geese.

To Roast a Swan (1)

Take 2 lb rump steak - chop it fine and season it well with spice, and add a slice of butter; then stuff with the above, taking care to sew the bird up carefully, and let it be tied tightly on the spit so that the gravy may not escape. Enclose the breast of the swan in a meal paste. Afterwards cover the whole bird with paper well greased with butter. A ¼ hour before it is taken up, remove the paper and paste. Baste well with butter and flour till it is brown and frothy. A swan of 15 lb weight will require 2¼ hours roasting with a fire not too fierce. To be served up with gravy and redcurrant jelly. The swan is not be skinned.
Mrs Garden, 1847

MrsBoyfield's way to Pickle a Ham

Pour on your Ham a pint of Good Vinegar, let it lay 2 days, then rub it even with 1 pound of Brown Sugar, 1 pound of Common Salt, 1 oz of Bay Salt, half an oz of salt Petre, let it remain in this pickle 3 weeks often turning.
Elizabeth Hicks: late 18th century

To Roast a Swan (2)

Take three pounds of beef, beat fine in a mortar
Put it into the swan (that is when you've caught her).
Some pepper, salt, mace, some nutmeg, an onion,
Will heighten the flavour in gorman'd opinion.
Then tie it up tight with a small piece of tape,
That the gravy and other things may not escape.
A meal paste, rather stiff, should be laid on the breast,
And some whited brown paper should cover the rest.
Fifteen minutes, at least, ere the swan you take down,
Put the paste off the bird, that the breast may get brown.'
Mrs Garden, 1847

Mrs Wade's Way to Roast a Pig

The pig to be layd down to the fire, and when it is dryd have a tea kettle of boiling water and keep pouring some on it till it is almost enough then baste it with some butter till it is quite so, then eat it as fast as you can.
Elizabeth Hicks: late 18th century

**This sounds like a joke, but it is a succulent way of dealing with a small sucking pig.*

Mrs Kent's Hashed Calves Head

Boil the Head quite tender and cut it in small pieces, fry it of a fine brown, then put it into a pint of strong gravy and let it stew slowly until the gravy is sufficiently reduced to serve it up in then put it into a deep dish and put crumbs of bread all over the top and salamander it till quite brown. Beat up the brains with yolks of two Eggs and fry them and forst meat balls. Garnish with Barberries and Lemon. Make the Gravy as follows: Put the beef in a stew pan with about 3 ounces of Butter well floured, 3 or 4 Cloves, Mace, Pepper & Salt to your taste Nutmeg and 2 anchovies, Onions, Thyme and a Bunch of Sweet Herbs keep stirring it over the fire till the Gravy is all drawn out of the Meat then add a full pint of boiling water and let it simmer till quite savory strain it off and put 2 Glasses of Madeira and some Cayenne Pepper.
Elizabeth Hicks: late 18th century

To Make Potted Beef

Take the Mouse piece or the tenderest part of your beef that comes in. Cut it in thin slices without any fat and put it in an earthen pot and between every layer of meat sprinkle a little cloves mace nutmegs pepper and salt beat fine add a little water over the beef with a thin slice of beef suet on the top of the beef before you bake it tie it close and put it in the oven after the bread is drawn and let it stand till the oven is cold then take of all the fat then beat it fine and add the gravy to it a little at a time put it in the cups with clarified butter.

Elizabeth Hicks: late 18th century

To Collar Beef

Take beef and season it with salt, pepper & spice and put in a round with a pint of Claret, then roll it up, tape and bake it in this liquor with brown bread.

Elizabeth Hicks: late 18th century

Mrs Colchester's Way to Hash Calves Head

Boil the Head an hour, & a quarter, then cut it into small pieces put it into a stew pan with a pint of good Veal or Beef gravy, a little Lemmon peel, a little Mace, a tea cup full of Cream, a spoonfull of White Wine and a little Catsup.

Elizabeth Hicks: late 18th century

Jugged Hare or Pheasant

Clean a hare or pheasant, and joint a hare. Put in a large earthenware jar or casserole and put in water to come half- way up. Add parsley, thyme and cloves, cover and simmer gently for as long as you like in the oven. Add a little more water during cooking to keep it moist, and put in a wineglass of port just before the end of cooking. Cook jacket potatoes in the same oven, and serve with buttered mashed parsnips.

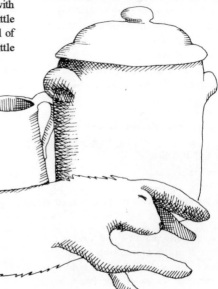

CHAPTER 4

Sweet Puddings and Pies

The English have always had a taste for something sweet, and old recipe books are packed with recipes for sweet finishes to a meal. As befits corn-growing areas, there are many favourite pies and puddings to stretch out fresh fruit and the more precious dried fruit. Apples and plums were always popular, the small warden pears, and wild blackberries and elderberries. In the summer, red- and white-currants appeared, cherries, gooseberries and raspberries, but there is no mention of blackcurrants or strawberries until the 19th century. Honey and sugar were used for sweetening and large quantities of spices.

Custards were a favourite sweet dish made with cream and eggs, often flavoured with rosewater or orange-flower water, or with almonds. Various whips were made with isinglass (used like gelatine), often with the juice of lemons or bitter Seville oranges. White wine, brandy and sherry were often used, and in Elizabethan times a sack posset was popular, made from sack (dry wine rather similar to sherry) thickened with sugar and eggs zabaglione or sabayon, but with the addition of cream. Another great favourite was syllabub, originally made by milking the cow directly into cider or beer or wine so that a frothy cream was formed. Gradually this changed to a thick mixture of cream, wine and brandy whipped together, and even this finally became a topping to cake and evolved into today's trifle.

Essex Raspberry Syllabub

8 oz raspberries; 2 oz sugar; 2 tablespoons rose water; ½ pint double cream; 7½ fl. oz. sweet white wine.

Bruise half the raspberries with a wooden spoon and leave the rest whole. Sprinkle with half the sugar and the rose water. Whip cream fairly stiff. Gradually add the remaining sugar and wine, whisking all the time so that the cream stands up in soft peaks. Add about half the cream to the raspberries and mix well. Then fold in the rest of the cream until streaked pale pink. Pile into glasses and chill.

Norfolk Syllabub

Scant ¼ pint white wine; 1 tablespoon sherry; 2 tablespoons brandy; 1 lemon or 1 bitter (Seville) orange; 2 oz caster sugar; ½ pint double cream.

Put the wine, sherry and brandy into a basin. Peel the lemon or orange very thinly, and squeeze out the juice. Put the peel and the juice into the wine mixture. Leave overnight, and remove the peel. Stir in the sugar until it dissolves. Add the cream and whip until the mixture forms soft peaks. Put into four tall glasses. This syllabub will hold its shape for 12 hours.

Suffolk Syllabub

Rub the rind of a lemon on ¼ lb sugar till well flavoured. Put the sugar into a basin, add a glass each of cooking sherry and brandy, and when the sugar melts pour in ½ pint of cream, stirring the whole time, and whisk till the mixture thickens. Pour into individual glasses and leave overnight in a cool place. Use the next day.

Solid Syllabub

Take the juice and peel of 2 lemons add to it a gill of Sherry sweeten it to your taste, boil 1 oz of Isinglass in three quarters of a pint of water and mix it with the Whisk then add to it a pint of Good thick cream and stir in until it begins to thicken then put it in your moulds.

Elizabeth Hicks: late 18th century

Hasty Pudding

A pint of milk, 2 spoonfuls of flour, mix these together, set it over the fire. Boil it into a smooth paste sweet it to your taste. Put in a little nutmeg, when almost Cold put in 5 Eggs & a small piece of Butter. Butter your pans and bake them three quarters of an hour. You may eat them with a Wine Sauce if you please.

Elizabeth Hicks: late 18th century

Rice Pudding

Six ounces of the flour of Rice put into a quart of milk let it boil till it is thick stirring it all the time put into a pan in half a pound of fresh butter and a quarter of a pound of Sugar when it is cool grate in a nutmeg, 6 eggs with 2 spoonfuls of Sack. Beat and stir them altogether lay a thin puff paste at the bottom of the Dish.

Elizabeth Hicks: late 18th century

Burnt Cream

Make a rich Custard without Sugar, boil it in some lemon peel, when cold sift sugar over it burn the top with a Salamander.

Elizabeth Hicks: late 18th century

Mrs Strutt's Ground Rice Pudding (Boxford)

Two Ozs of Rice, 1 pint of Milk, add 4 eggs, a little Beef Suet, a few currants, a little Brandy sweeten it to your taste. Bake it in a puff paste.

Elizabeth Hicks: late 18th century

A Hunting Pudding

One pound of jar raisins half a pound of flour half a pound of suet 4 eggs half a nutmeg half a wine glass of brandy and just milk enough to mix the ingredients up should boil 5 hours.

Elizabeth Hicks: late 18th century

Mrs Kent's Spanish Puffs

Take 1 pint of spring water with 3 ounces of Butter, the rind of 1 Lemon cut fine, then boil it altogether 5 minutes then take fine flour and stir it till it becomes a thick paste, then take 6 eggs only 3 whites, work them well.

Elizabeth Hicks: late 18th century

Cream Pancakes

One pint of Cream half a pound of melted butter, 6 eggs half the white, mix it well together with some flour it must be pretty thin batter.

Elizabeth Hicks: late 18th century

Lemon Cream

A pint of water the juice of 4 lemons beat up 4 eggs 10 ounces of loaf sugar a little lemon peal set all these onto the fire together stirring them till they are just ready to boil take them off the fire stir them a little while then put them into your glasses.

Elizabeth Hicks: late 18th century

Currant Cream

Strip the currants, bruise them and strain them and take the clear juice and sweeten it with fine sugar, then take as much cream as juice, mix them in a Bason and beat them as eggs with a spoon. As the froth rises put it into little Glasses. Do Raspberries the same.

Elizabeth Hicks: late 18th century

Mrs Snow's Mince Pies

One Lemon, the weight of it in Currants, Sugar, and Suet, add Brandy if you please.

Elizabeth Hicks: late 18th century

Suffolk Lemon Solid

Warm a pint of milk with the grated rind of 2 lemons, 6 oz sugar and ½ oz powdered gelatine. Heat it until the sugar and galatine have melted, stirring well. Add the juice of 2 lemons and stir until the curd separates. Put into a bowl and turn out when set. A 'solid' could be eaten with cream or with fresh or stewed fruit.

Bungay Fruit Fool (1823)

Bruise 1 pint scarlet strawberries, 1 pint raspberries and pass them through a hair sieve. Mix them with ½ lb fine sugar and 1 tablespoon orange flower water. Boil up 1½ pints cream and stir till it is cold. Beat the fruit pulp and the cold cream together and stir them till they are well mixed. Put some fine strawberries for decoration.

Boiled Batter

Mix 6 oz plain flour and a pinch of salt and add 3 beaten eggs and about ¾ pint of milk to make a creamy batter. Leave to stand for an hour and put into a well greased basin. Cover with a floured cloth and boil for 1¼ hours. This batter pudding was sometimes served with gravy before a meal, or could be eaten with butter and brown sugar after the main course. Dried fruit can be put into the batter, or fresh fruit, before it is boiled.

Apple Dowdy (Essex)

Take about 1½ lb of apples, slices of stale bread and butter, a little nutmeg, 1 gill of water, 1 gill of golden syrup, 2 ounces of Demerara sugar. Well butter a deep baking tin or pie dish. Line the bottom with the thin slices of bread and butter. Peel, core, and slice the apples, and nearly fill the dish with them. Grate over a little nutmeg. Now mix the syrup and water, pour it in over the apples. Put the sugar in a layer over the top, and cover all with more bread and butter. Cover the top over with a tin plate or lid, and bake in a moderate oven about 2 hours. Then loosen the edges with a knife, put on a hot dish, and serve with sugar and cream; or it can be served in the dish it is cooked in.

Norfolk Pudding

4 oz plain flour; Pinch of salt; ½ pint milk; 1 egg; 1 lb apples; 2 oz sugar; 2 oz dried fruit; ½ oz cooking fat or dripping.
Sieve the flour and salt together and mix to a batter with the milk and egg. Peel and core the apples and cut in thin slices. Put the fat into a pie dish, add the apples and heat in the oven at 400°F, 200°C, Gas Mark 6 for 5 minutes. Sprinkle with sugar and dried fruit and pour on the batter mixture. Bake at 450°F, 230°C, Gas Mark 8 for 30 minutes. Serve hot, sprinkled with a little sugar.
***Crisp eating apples taste best in this pudding, and keep their shape well.*

Lemon Sponge from Tendring Hall (Essex)

Dissolve 1½ oz isinglass in 1 pint water. Add the juice of 4 lemons with white wine and sugar to taste. Whip together until very thick, then put into moulds.

Sir Charles Rowley's Plum Pudding (1857)

Cut ½ lb good beef suet very large. Mix ½ lb raisins, 7 oz flour, 2 oz sugar, a little salt. Stir in suet and bind with 2 well-beaten eggs. Put into a cloth wrung out of hot water and floured, and boil. This is a Suffolk recipe, and needs boiling about 3 hours.

Ipswich Almond Pudding (1741)

1½ oz breadcrumbs; ¾ pint cream; ¼ lb ground almonds; A little rose or orange flower water; 4 eggs; 2 oz castor sugar.
Make the cream hot and pour it on the crumbs, then stir in the sugar, almonds and flavouring. Beat up your yolks and 2 whites of eggs, mix well with the other ingredients, and pour into a buttered pie dish, putting a few little pieces of butter at the top. Let it bake for half an hour in a slow oven.

Sandringham Christmas Pudding

A recipe given to Hon. Albert Petre, a friend of the Royal Family

1 lb eggs; 1 lb plain flour; 1 lb white breadcrumbs; 1 lb suet; 1 lb currants; 1 lb raisins; 1 lb sultanas; 1 lb demerara sugar; ¼ lb mixed peel; ½ oz salt; 1 dessertspoon mixed spice; 1 wineglass brandy.

Beat eggs and mix all ingredients except brandy thoroughly with hands then stir in brandy. Cover with a thick cloth and leave for 12 hours. Put into buttered basins, cover with 3 layers of greaseproof paper within bowls and completely cover with floured and buttered cloth. Boil 21 hours and a further 3 hours day of eating having, of course, removed damp cloth after first boiling, also top layer of paper and replaced with clean pudding cloth.

Norfolk Raspberry Rice

For this, a pudding-basin is greased and 3 tablespoonfuls of good, lightly cooked raspberry jam is laid in the bottom, then 4 heaped tablespoonfuls of well-cooked rice are put in, spread with more raspberry jam, and the basin then filled with rice, covered with a cloth and steamed for 1 hour. It is essential that the rice shall have been boiled in milk and cooked until it has absorbed the milk. Custard, made very sweet, is served with this dish.
Mrs Arthur Webb

Apple Johns (Norfolk)

Select apples of an even size. Peel and core carefully and into each cavity left by the removal of the core put ½ teaspoonful of brown sugar, and a small knob of butter topped with a clove. Roll out a simple short pastry, cut into pieces 5 inches square, and in the centre of each square place an apple. Pinch the corners of the pastry together over the top of the apple, place carefully in a pan, bake for ½ an hour. When they come to table, the fruit in the Apple Johns should be seen through the four openings in the pastry.
Mrs Arthur Webb.

Mrs Townley's Fulbourn Apple Pudding

Peel 2 dozen russetts, remove the cores and cut them in slices. Put them into a deep saucepan with 4 oz butter, the rind of 2 lemons, 12 oz pounded sugar and 1 lb apricot jam. Toss the whole over a slow stove fire until the apples begin to dissolve and then set them aside to cool. Next, line a good-sized basin with some light-made suet paste. Fill this with the prepared apples - place a covering of paste on the top and fasten it down securely and steam it for about 2 hours. It may also be served up with some warm apricot jam poured over it. This apple preparation is also best for apple Charlottes or for apples served with rice, or whipped cream.
Mrs Garden, 1847

Fresh Plum Pudding and Audley End Sauce (Essex)

1 egg; butter; flour; sugar; ½ lb small ripe plums; Soft brown sugar;
Sauce
2 oz cornflour; 1 pint milk; 2 oz butter; 1½ oz sugar; 1 egg; ½ gill top milk or cream. 1 tablespoon moist brown sugar.
Weigh the egg and weigh out the equivalent in butter, flour and sugar. Remove stones from plums and cut them in half. Cream butter and sugar, add beaten egg and flour. Spread a layer of this sponge mixture in a greased oven dish, add the plums face down and sprinkle lightly with sugar, then add the rest of the sponge mixture. Bake at 350°F, 180°C, Gas Mark 4 for 30 minutes until golden and firm. Make the sauce by mixing cornflour with a little water then cooking gently for 5 minutes with the boiling milk, butter and sugar. Gradually whisk in the egg and top milk or cream. Put sauce into a buttered dish, sprinkle sugar on top and caramelise under a hot grill. Serve sauce either hot or cold.

John Simpson's Barberry Tart (1805)

Sheet a tartpan with puff paste, put preserved barberries in and crossbar it. John Simpson was cook to the first Marquess of Buckingham at Gosfield Hall, Essex.

Manor House Marrow Pudding

Take 1 pint of breadcrumbs, ½ pint of currants, ½ lb of raisins, lemon and orange peel, ½ lb suet cut very fine - the marrow out of a round of beef bone is the best if you have it. Mix all together then take a small piece of puff paste and line the dish you intend to bake it in with the paste. Fill the dish half full of mixture. Take 6 eggs beaten well, as much sugar as will sweeten to your taste, 1 quart of new milk and mix with the eggs, nutmeg according to fancy. Put it in ½ glass of brandy. Pour this custard in the dish with the other mixture. It will take 1¼ hours to bake. From the Manor House, Brentwood.
Mrs Garden, 1847

Kiss Me Quick Pudding

2 eggs and their weight in flour, sugar and butter; 2 tablespoons raspberry jam; 1 small teaspoon soda bicarb
All beaten up. Steam it 1 hour and ½.
Mrs Garden, 1847

Dripping Puddings

The weight of 3 eggs in their shells in dripping; ½ teacup currants; tablespoon powdered sugar; flour to thicken.

Beat up the eggs, add the sugar and currants also the dripping (melted if too hard); beat up all together, thickening it with flour, but do not make it too stiff or they will not be light. Bake in small tins.
Mrs Garden, 1847

Mary Eaton's Strawberries in Wine (1823)

This recipe comes from Bungay in Suffolk. Hull the fruit and put in a wide-necked jar. Sprinkle with a little fine sugar over each layer. Fill up with fine sherry, Madeira, or better still a bottle of home-made orange wine. This was a form of preserve when it was made, but it is excellent today if kept in the refrigerator for a day or two until needed.

Apricot Pie

Coddle 6 large apricots very tender. Break them very small, sweeten them to your taste. When they are cold add 6 eggs (only 2 whites) well beaten. Mix them well together with a pint of good cream. Lay a puff paste all over ye dish and pour in your ingredients. Bake it ½ an hour. Don't let the oven be too hot. When it is enough, throw a little fine sugar over it, and send it to the table hot.
Mrs Garden, 1847

Southwold Treacle Custard (1832)

Grease a deep plate and put in shortcrust. Beat up an egg and warm syrup (2 table-spoons) until it is liquid. Beat up the egg and syrup and pour into pastry. Bake in a slow oven until golden brown. Eat cold, when the mixture will set like a jelly.

French Dumpling

Half a pound of bread grated fine half a pound of suet half a pound of currants clean washed, 3 eggs, 3 spoonfuls of sugar, 3 spoonfuls of white wine, some nutmeg and a little salt, mix all together put them into cloths. This quantity will make eight dumplings. Boil them 20 minutes, make your sauce of a little white wine and sugar put into a little melted butter.
Elizabeth Hicks: late 18th century

Mrs Cole's Dutch Flummery

Put 1 oz and half of isinglass into a bason with a pint of boiling water, let stand 12 hours. Add a pint of white wine, the yolks of 6 eggs well beaten the juice of a large lemon and the peal of 1 sweeten it to your taste keep it stirring all the time then strain it through a jelly bag.
Elizabeth Hicks: late 18th century

Colchester Pudding

Take 1 pint of milk, 2 ounces of tapioca, the rind of 1 lemon, vanilla, 2 tablespoonsful of caster sugar, stewed fruit, custard, whites of 2 eggs. Put the milk in a clean pan on the fire, pare the lemon rind very thinly and put it in. Bring the milk slowly to the boil, strain out the rind, and sprinkle in the tapioca. Simmer this very slowly in the milk till it is soft and creamy. Keep the lid on, but stir it frequently. Then add sugar and vanilla to taste. Pour it on to the fruit; it should be just thick enough to flow over it nicely. If too thick, add a little more milk. Let this get cold, then pour over a good boiled custard. Lastly, beat up the whites of the eggs to a very stiff froth; sweeten with the caster sugar, and add a few drops of vanilla. Colour the froth a pale pink with a few drops of cochineal. Heap it over the top of the custard.

Raspberry Sponge (Essex)

Take the whites of 4 eggs and beat them to a firm froth. Take about 1 lb of good fresh ripe raspberries, stalk them, mash them thoroughly, and sweeten them to taste with sifted sugar. Then gradually beat them into the whisked whites, a little at a time, so that the sponge keeps stiff. Pile it up in a glass dish.

Toffee Apple Pudding (Norfolk)

½ lb flour; 6 oz suet; 1½ lb apples; 6 tea-spoonfuls brown sugar
For the toffee
2 oz butter; 2 oz brown sugar.
Peel, core, and cut up the apples. Make the suet crust and roll out thin. Instead of a basin, take a pie-dish and put in the 2 oz of butter and 2 oz of brown sugar, taking care that the bottom and sides of the dish are well covered with the mixture. Line with the thin suet crust, pile in the apples, add the sugar, cover with the remaining crust, put into the oven, bake for 1¼ hours. If the dish has been greased carefully with butter and sugar, this pudding will turn out with a rich, sauce-like mixture covering it.
Mrs Arthur Webb

Norfolk Treacle Tart

1 shortcrust pastry case; 6 tablespoons golden syrup; Grated rind of 1 lemon; ½ oz of butter; 3 tablespoons single cream; 2 eggs.
Use about 10 oz shortcrust pastry to line a sandwich tin or flan ring. Warm the syrup until thin but not hot. Gradually add the lemon rind, butter, cream and beaten eggs. Pour into the pastry case and bake in a moderate oven (350°F, 180°C, Gas Mark 4) for 45 minutes.

Norfolk Marrow Tart (Million Pie)

8 oz shortcrust pastry; 2 oz jam; 1 lb vegetable marrow; 1 egg; Pinch of ground nutmeg; 1½ tablespoons sugar.
Line a tin with the pastry, keeping the trimmings to decorate the top of the tart. Spread with a thin layer of jam. Boil the marrow until soft and place in a colander to remove all the liquid. When cold, add a well-beaten egg, and nutmeg. Beat together with a fork and put in the bottom of the flan. Sprinkle a little nutmeg over the top. Decorate with strips of pastry. Bake at 400°F, 180°C, Gas Mark 6 for 10-15 minutes until turning brown. Continue at 350°F, 180°C, Gas Mark 4 for 10 minutes until the pastry is golden. Serve hot or cold.
**This was a great favourite until quite recently, when marrow was considered a fruit, rather than a vegetable. Currants or raisins could also be added to the filling.

Another version was simply made with marrow slices cooked with sugar, raisins and water in a pie dish until tender, then covered with a pastry crust. The dish is sometimes known as Million Pie, a 'million' being a sort of marrow. Sometimes the marrow was combined with pork in a savoury pie.

Baked Apple Pudding

Take 6 apples cut small and simmer them in a pan with lemon peel, lump sugar and cinnamon and cloves according to your taste. Boil a lemon whole till quite soft, beat it up and mix it with the apples. Take 6 yolks and 4 whites of eggs, beat them up and when the apples are quite cold, stir them together. Then have it baked with a paste round it. Strew almonds on the top. This recipe and variations on it, appear in a number of old manuscript books, but Mrs Garden's version is the easiest and clearest. Possibly it was copied from a popular book or magazine of the period.

Mrs Garden, 1847

Stone Cream

Cover the bottom of a glass dish about an inch thick with apricot jam. Plum or Strawberry will do. To a pint of cream put a little white powdered sugar and just enough isinglass to make a very little stiff. Nearly boil it and when the isinglass is dissolved strain it. When nearly cold pour over the preserves in the glass dish. You can put any ornaments you please on the top.

Mrs Garden, 1847

Mrs Kent's Lemon Pudding (Ipswich)

One large lemon grate the rind and take all the juice. Add a quarter of a pound of loaf sugar and 2 of clarified butter. When all these are well mixed and quite cold put in 4 eggs well beaten, bake them in puff paste in a quick Oven.

Elizabeth Hicks: late 18th century

Potatoe Pudding

One pound of Boiled Potatoes, a Quarter of a pound of Butter, a Quarter of a Pound of Sugar, half a Pound of Currants, & 4 eggs, Wine and Nutmeg to your taste.

Elizabeth Hicks: late 18th century

Bread Pudding

Grate a penny loaf, pour a pint of boiling milk, then stir it up with a pound of butter and 4 eggs. Grate the peel of a lemon, and some of juice, then sweeten it to your taste.

Elizabeth Hicks: late 18th century

Rice Pudding

Two ounces of Ground Rice, a pint of Milk. Boil them together, then add a little Beef suet with a few currants, a spoonful of Brandy, sweeten it to your taste.

Elizabeth Hicks: late 18th century

Norfolk Apple Pie

12 oz shortcrust pastry; 2 lb cooking apples; 1 oz butter; 1 tablespoon granulated sugar; 2 tablespoons orange marmalade; 1 tablespoon currants.

Line a deep 8 inch pie plate with half the pastry. Peel, core and slice the apples and cook them without any water, adding the small knob of butter to prevent burning. When they are soft, stir in the sugar and beat them to a pulp. Pour half of this into the pastry case, spread the marmalade over and sprinkle on the currants. Spread the remaining apple pulp on the top. Make a lid from the other piece of pastry and put on top. Trim and decorate the edges. Bake 400°F, 200°C, Gas Mark 6 for 15 minutes, then reduce heat to 350°F, 180°C, Gas Mark 4.

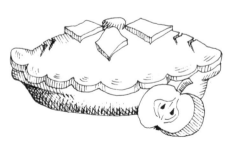

CHAPTER 5

Bread, Cakes and Biscuits

In this sunny dry corner of England, the corn harvest was an important season. Although today's church Harvest Festival is a Victorian invention, the harvest was celebrated throughout the country by suppers or horkeys at which masters and servants met to give thanks for the crops which provided their livelihood and so much of their vital food. A corn dolly or goddess was made from the last sheaves in the field, to be treasured until the next year's sowing, and these can occasionally be seen at church harvest festivals. In Suffolk, straw stacks were thatched and decorated with other corn shapes.

Bread was commonly baked at home, originally on the hearth or in a covered iron pot over which hot embers could be heaped. Later, bread ovens were built into farmhouses and cottages, and baking day had its set ritual. A fire had to be lit and kept going for some time until the brick oven was hot; when the hot ashes were raked out the oven was ready for bread-making which needed high heat. Food which needed lower heat might be placed in the oven as the heat rose for bread-baking, but more often a variety of pies, milk puddings and custards were baked in the 'dying oven', and many old recipes specify that dishes may be cooked 'when the bread is drawn' or 'with the small bread' - in other words once the main batch of bread had been baked, and the smaller items were being prepared.

Rusks were popular in East Anglia, baked like scones, then split and baked again until crisp. Some recipes are made with yeast, others without. Yeast was also the common raising agent for cakes before the discovery of chemical agents and the later preparation of self-raising flour in the 19th century. The yeast which was used was ale yeast or barm, much sloppier than today's compressed variety, and with a strong beer taste, but it worked well in fruity spicecakes. When spongecakes were made, the raising agent was air incorporated by hard beating, often specified as 'three hours'. A variety of shortbread-type biscuits was prepared and fruit shortcakes made from ends of pastry. Special harvest cakes were sometimes of the yeast variety, but more often a form of lardy cake in which lard, sugar and dried fruit were worked into layers into bread dough. Lard was used for these simple cakes as it was readily available after pig-killing and butter was expensive except on farms where cattle were kept.

Harvest Time

A health-drinking catch was drunk in Norfolk (1827) at the end of harvest supper just before parting:

> *'Now supper is over, and all things are past,*
> *Here's our mistress's good health in a full flowing glass;*
> *She is a good mistress, she provides us good cheer;*
> *Here's our mistress's good health, boys - come drink **half** your beer.*
> *She is a good mistress, she provides us good cheer;*
> *Here's our mistress's good health, boys - come drink **off** your beer.'*

During the time the catch is going round, the whole party are standing and, with the exception of the drinker, they join in the chorus. The glass circulates, beginning with the 'Lord', in regular succession through the company, and after it is handed to the harvestmen of bygone days. If the drinker is taken off his guard, he pays a forfeit, and if one of the chorus misplaces the words 'half' and 'off' (a frequent occurrence at the end of the evening) he also pays a forfeit. After this song comes one to the master:

> *'Here's a health to our master, the Lord of the feast.*
> *God bless his endeavours and send him increase,*
> *And send him good crops, that we may meet another year;*
> *Here's our master's good health, boys - come drink **half** your beer.*
> *God send him good crops, boys - come drink **off** your beer.'*

The catch is sometimes carried on with other members of the family, with verses made up on the spur of the moment.

Folk Lore Cakes

All country areas have their superstitions, and love divinations were practised by many Norfolk maidens with the aid of special cakes.

Dumb Cake

St. Mark's Eve was the time for Dumb Cake, so called because of the rigid silence which attends its manufacture. It is a 'dreaming bread' prepared by unmarried females with traditional ingredients:

> *An egg-shell full of salt,*
> *An egg-shell full of wheatmeal,*
> *An egg-shell full of barleymeal.*

The cake must be baked before the fire a little before 12 o'clock at night. The maker of the cake must be quite alone, must be fasting, and not a word must be spoken. By some girls it is believed that exactly at 12 o'clock the sweetheart will come in and turn the cake. But the more general formula is to cut the mystic viand, when baked, into three divisions, a part of each to be eaten and the remainder to be put under the pillow. When the clock strikes 12, the damsels must go upstairs backwards and jump into bed, keeping a profound silence whatever may happen. Those who are to be married, or are full of hope, fancy they see visions of their future husbands hurrying after them; while those who are to live and die old maids see nothing at all.

Wedding Cake

A common flat cake of flour, water, currants, etc. is made, and a wedding-ring and a sixpence are put therein. When the company are about to retire on the wedding day, the cake is broken and distributed amongst the unmarried females. She who gets the ring in her portion of the cake will shortly be married, and she who gets the sixpence will die an old maid.

The Norfolk Garland, 1872

Suffolk Rusks

8 oz self-raising flour; Pinch of salt; 3 oz butter; 1 egg; Milk or water to mix..

Sieve the flour and salt together. Rub in the butter lightly and mix with the beaten egg and just enough milk or water to make a smooth dough. Roll out lightly 1 inch thick and cut in 2½ inch rounds. Bake at 450°F. 230°C, Gas Mark 8 for 10 minutes. Remove from the oven and split in half. Put on baking sheets with the cut sides upward. Bake at 375°F, 190°C, Gas Mark 5 for 15 minutes until crisp and golden. Cool and serve with butter and cheese or jam. These rusks store well in a tin.

Suffolk Rusks Another Way

This is a rich version of the Suffolk rusk made in Woodbridge, which should be well dried out. The rusks are good for breakfast, spread with butter. Rub 4 oz lard and 4 oz butter into 1½ lb plain flour with ¾ oz baking powder. Mix with ¼ pint of milk, 1 beaten egg, ½ oz of sugar and a good pinch of salt. Roll out ½ in. thick and cut in 2 in. rounds. Leave to stand for half an hour, then bake at 400°F, 200°C, Gas Mark 6 for 20 minutes. Cool slightly, split in two and put split side up on baking tins. Bake in the sam heat oven for 10 minutes until golden. Cool on wire racks.

Fourses or Harvest Cakes

Use the same recipe as Suffolk Rusks, and to each 1 lb of dough add an ounce of lard, sugar and raisins. Add a sprinkling of spice. Make into buns about 4 inches across. These cakes are eaten at 4 o'clock, accompanied by sugar beer. Fourses actually contain less fat and fruit, and in olden days when the family and farmhands fed in the kitchen, the richer cake was eaten at the family end of the table. It is thought that the name originated from the round or square cakes which were cut lightly across, twice at right angles, to divide the cakes into four, and also because it was the custom to eat these cakes at the 4 o'clock break.

Sophia Barnardiston's Rusks (1830)

2 lb flour, 2 spoonfuls of yeast, the whites of 2 eggs. Beat to a froth, melt a ¼ of a lb of butter, 3 lumps of sugar, in a pint of milk, let it stand till almost cold, and mix them all together as you make bread. Set it before the fire to rise. Make them in *very* small rolls, half an hour will bake them, and before they are quite done, pull them asunder and put them into the oven again till they become of a light brown colour. The Barnardiston family came from the Clare area of Suffolk.

Brotherly Love (Suffolk)

Take about a pound of bread dough, roll out into ½ inch strip. Dab on, in small pieces, 1 oz lard, and sprinkle over 2 oz sugar. Roll up the strip into the shape of a large Chelsea bun. Bake in a hot oven 400°F, 200°C, Gas Mark 6 for about half an hour.

Norfolk Shortcakes

8 oz plain flour; ½ teaspoon baking powder 4 oz butter or lard; 1½ oz granulated sugar; 1½ oz currants; 2½ fl. oz water.

Sieve the flour with the baking powder and rub in 2 oz of the fat. Divide the rest of the fat into three portions; also the currants and sugar. Mix the flour into a pliable paste with the cold water and roll it out into a long strip. Spread this with dabs of fat and sprinkle with sugar and currants. Fold into three layers, give the paste a half turn and repeat this process twice more. Roll out about quarter of an inch thick, cut into 24 2½ inch rounds or squares and bake at 400°F, 200°C, Gas Mark 6 for 15 minutes until golden-brown. Dredge with castor sugar when cooked. These were often made with the ends of pastry after a baking session.

Mrs Strutt's Good Cheese-cake with Curd (Boxford)

A pound & half of Curd (four quarts of milk make that quantity) when it is well drained, five ozs of Butter, beat these in a mortar till all look like Butter, six Eggs with half the whites, a little beaten Mace, two spoonfuls of thick Cream and half a pound of fine sugar a quarter of an hour bake them in puff paste in a quick oven. Put in what currants you think proper.

Elizabeth Hicks: late 18th century

Norfolk Shortcakes (Another Way)

1 lb plain flour; ½ lb lard; 1 teaspoon baking powder; 3 oz granulated sugar; 3 oz currants; Salt.

Sift the flour and baking powder and a pinch of salt into a basin. Work 6 oz of lard to a crumb with the flour. Pour in a little water gradually. Make into a paste and roll out ½ inch thick. Smear a little lard over the surface of the pastry, then sprinkle on a layer of sugar and a few currants. Fold and repeat the rolling and sprinkling four times. Cut into small rounds, bake in a hot oven for 15 minutes. Properly made these shortcakes are very flaky and, with a little fine sugar sprinkled over the top of them when straight from the oven they are very appetizing.

Mrs Arthur Webb

Norfolk Fair Buttons

8 oz sugar; 8 oz plain flour; 6 oz butter; 1 egg.

Stir together the sugar and flour and rub in the butter. Mix to a paste and roll out thinly. Cut into rounds and bake at 350°F. 180°C, Gas Mark 4 for 10 minutes. This is a form of shortbread, which can also be flavoured with ginger. The biscuits were traditionally eaten at the Tombland Easter Fair in Norwich and at Yarmouth Easter Fair and are still often available from commercial bakers.

Miss Jarry's Hollow Biscuits

Pour 2 teacupsfull of boiling Water upon 2 ounces of Butter. Pour it upon the flour hot, take 1 cupfull of Water, an egg, 2 spoonsfull of yeast, as much flour as will make them stiff: they must not be cut round the edges. Bake them 2 hours in a slack oven, the above quantity makes about 4 dozen.

** Norfolk Hollows, sometimes known as Norfolk Nobs, were like yeast rolls which were baked one day, then left overnight and baked again so they were very hard and crisp. They are similar to the celebrated Dorset Knob.

Norfolk Rusks

In the earlier years of this century no Norfolk breakfast would be complete without buttered rusks. Norfolk rusks differ from the Suffolk variety in having no egg.

Mrs Wootton's Mince Pies

To a pound of Meat, put one pound & Qr of suet, three pound of currants, half an oz of Mace, a Qr of an Oz of Cloves, two large Nutmegs, three Lemons & the peel, eight or ten large apples, half a pint of brandy & half a pint of wine.

Elizabeth Hicks: late 18th century

Mrs Colchester's Good Plumb Cake

Take 3 pound of flour a pound and a half of butter rub 1 pound into your flour and put the rest into a quarter of a pint of milk make it only hot enough to melt the butter. Take 12 eggs, 2 spoonfuls of yeast, beat them well together and strain them through a sieve and mix your cake beating it well set by the fire till risen and when the oven is ready put in 3 pounds of currants a pound of sugar a little spice a cup of brandy and half a pound of almonds and orange juice.

Elizabeth Hicks: late 18th century

Ginger Bread

Treacle 2 pounds, sugar 1 pound, of butter 1 pound. The sugar and butter melted together over a slow fire, a few Carraway seeds and candid orange peel cut fine 2 ozs of ginger a glass of brandy and flour sufficient to make it into a paste and bake them quick.

Elizabeth Hicks: late 18th century

Mrs Wootton's Ginger Bread Cakes

Three quarters of a pound of flour, half a pound of treacle, ¼ lb of sugar, quarter of butter, a quarter of an oz of Ginger a little Brandy or Wine & Lemon peal.

Elizabeth Hicks: late 18th century

Mrs Head's Pound Cake (Ipswich)

To 1 pound of flour, three quarters of a pound of Lump sugar beat fine and sifted, mix them together and lay before the fire half an hour, beat well 9 Eggs with 6 of the whites, 1 pound of Butter out of which squeeze all the water, then beat it well with your hand mixing the Eggs to it by degrees, add the Flour and sweetmeats to your palate, add half a wineglass of Brandy. This will take an Hour mixing and baking 3 in a slow oven.

Elizabeth Hicks: late 18th century

Mrs Strutt's Ratiffee Cakes

Half a pound of Bitter Almonds, 1 pound of sugar, the whites of 2 eggs and a large spoonful of flour.

Elizabeth Hicks: late 18th century

Snaps

One pound & Qr of Flour, 1 pound of Treacle half a pound of sugar, half a pound of Butter 1 oz or half of ginger. Put the Sugar into the Flour & Ginger then Boil the Treakle and Butter Together and put it on hot and mix them up well and let them stand all night then roll them very thin and cut them in cakes.

Elizabeth Hicks: late 18th century

Mrs Grime's Rich Plumb Cake

One pound & half of Flour, a pound & half of Butter, 3 Qrs of a pound of Sugar, two pounds and half of Currants, 12 Eggs, 1 Nutmeg, a little Mace, 6 ozs of Almonds sliced, a little Brandy, as much candid peal as you please. Work the butter with your hand till it becomes Cream, then put in the Sugar & work it well, the Flour and the Yolks of the Eggs, then put in spice and Almonds, beat the Whites of the Eggs till they froth then put it into the rest keep it Working till it goes into the oven.

Elizabeth Hicks: late 18th century

Mrs Strutt's Common Plumb Cake

One pound & half of Flour, 1 pint & half of Milk, 2 spoonfuls of yeast, 2 pound of Currants, 5 Eggs, 1 pound of soft sugar, half a pound of Butter, 2 ozs of orange peel, a little nutmeg, mace & Brandy, the Butter must be melted and put in when the Cake rises

Elizabeth Hicks: late 18th century

Miss Ransom's Dish Bread

To 6 ozs of Flour put 6 oz of Lump Sugar with 4 eggs yolks and whites.

Elizabeth Hicks: late 18th century

God's Kitchels (Suffolk)

'Ask me a blessing and I will give you a kitchel' was a Suffolk saying connected with these cakes given to visiting godchildren by their godparents during the 12 days of Christmas. Use 1 lb puff pastry. Melt 2 oz butter and add ½ lb currants, 3 oz chopped candied peel, 2 oz ground almonds, ½ teaspoonful cinnamon and 1 teaspoonful nutmegs. Divide the pastry in two and roll each piece into a thin square. Moisten the edge all round with water and spread the filling evenly to within ½ in. of the edge. Cover with the second piece of pastry and press the edges well together. Then with the back of a knife mark the top of the pastry into divisions about 2 ins square but be careful not to cut through to the filling. Bake in a very hot oven for 25-30 minutes. Sprinkle with castor sugar and while still warm divide into little cakes as marked.

Sheet Lightning (Suffolk)

Spread thin slices of bread and butter with golden syrup. In some parts of Suffolk, the bread is fried in butter and allowed to become quite cold before spreading. Place each slice on an individual plate. Cover with a thick layer of whipped cream. Serve for dinner or high tea.

Suffolk Oaten Wafers

6 oz plain flour or 6 oz self-raising flour and take only half the baking powder; 1 teaspoon baking powder; ½ oz sugar; ½ teaspoon salt; 1½ oz rolled oats (porridge oats); 2 oz margarine; Enough milk to make dough.
First mix dry ingredients, then rub in fat with finger tips. Mix to a firm dough with a little milk. Knead lightly on a lightly floured board. Roll out thinly. Cut into rounds. Bake on a greased baking sheet, a little apart, in a moderately hot oven at 425°F, 220°C, Gas Mark 7 for about ¼ hour or till brown. Cool on a wire rack.

To Make Jumbles

Take 1 pound of Flour half a pound of Butter 12 ounces of sugar 4 Eggs 2 with whites and 2 without. To be made only with Hands and Dropt on Tins.
Elizabeth Hicks: late 18th century

To Make Jumbles Another Way

Half a pound of Flour, a Quarter of a pound of Butter rubbed into the Flour, 2 Eggs leaving out 1 White, a large spoonfull of yeast, the peal of a Lemon shread fine add a little Brandy or rosewater, make it into a paste and roll it in lump sugar and Bake them on tins.

Elizabeth Hicks: late 18th century

Suffolk Apple Cake

Equal quantities of apples and flour, half the quantity in fat (beef dripping is preferred). Add 3 tablespoons of sugar and 3 tablespoons of baking powder for 1 lb of flour, a pinch of salt and milk to mix. Rub fat into flour with baking powder and salt. Chop the pared apples finely, add the sugar, mix all into a firm dough with the milk. Make into a flat round cake ¼ in. thick. Bake on a tin for ¾ to 1 hour, split open, butter well and eat hot.

To Make Cheese Cakes

Take a quarter of a pound of Currants, a Qr of a pound of sugar a Qr of a pint of Cream the yolks of 4 eggs and 1 White, a Qr of a pound of Butter. Beat the Curd & Butter together, put in a small glass of Brandy, a little Mace, a little Nutmeg, you may grate a little lemon peel, stir all together, and put into puff paste.
Elizabeth Hicks: late 18th century

Lemon Cheesecakes

The yolks of 8 eggs, half a pound of sugar, 5 ounces of Butter, the juice of a large Lemon and the peel grated make them in nice crust. Bake them with small Bread.
Elizabeth Hicks: late 18th century

Suffolk Harvest Cake

1 lb white flour; 4 oz cornflour; 2 teaspoons baking powder; ½ teaspoon bicarbonate of soda; Pinch of powdered nutmeg; Pinch of powdered cinnamon; 1 oz finely crumbled yeast; 1 lb sugar; 8 oz lard; ½ pint milk; 2 eggs; 1 lb currants; 4 oz chopped candied lemon peel.

Sift together the flour, cornflour, baking powder, bicarbonate of soda, nutmeg and cinnamon. Rub in the crumbled yeast and stir in the sugar. Cut the lard into flakes and work into the dry ingredients. Finally stir in currants and candied peel until the ingredients are well blended. Put into two greased and lined 10-inch round tins and leave in a warm place for 30 minutes to rise. Bake at 350°F, 180°C, Gas Mark 4 for 2 hours.

Threadneedle Street Biscuits (1840)

Rub 3 oz butter into 2 lbs flour until it is fine. Work in 4 oz fine sugar and ½ teaspoon soda with fresh milk to mix. Roll out ½ in. thick and cut in squares or lozenges. Very slow oven till crisp. Always taken by stage coach on trips to European towns, by Dorothy Nevill, daughter of the Earl of Orford.

Coquilles

1 oz yeast; 2 oz sugar; 2 oz butter; 1 lb plain flour; ½ pint lukewarm water; 1 egg; Ground nutmeg.

Cream the yeast and sugar with a little of the water. Rub the butter into the flour and work in the egg and yeast mixture, flavouring with nutmeg. Add a little of the remaining water to make a soft dough. Leave in a warm place for 30 minutes to prove. Break into pieces about 2 oz weight, shape into rounds and prove again for 30 minutes. Bake at 425°F, 220°C, Gas Mark 7 for 20 minutes.

** These were a traditional Easter speciality and there was a street cry to advertise 'Hot penny coquilles, smoking all hot'. Fishermen's wives used cockle shells to mould small cakes before tin utensils were available, so it is possible this is how coquilles got their name. The Southend version is for small cakes baked in scallop shells..

Tunbridges Water Cakes

Take half a pound of flour, a Qr pound of dry powder Sugar 2 ozs of Butter, half an oz of Carraway Seeds a small cup of Water mix it to a light paste and roll'd out very thin, & prickt you cannot roll them in too little flour. Bake them on tins.

Elizabeth Hicks: late 18th century

Suffolk Buns

Rub 4 ounces of lard into a pound of flour; add a spoonful of salt, 2 tablespoonfuls of sugar and 3 tablespoonfuls of currants or caraway seeds. Mix the dry ingredients thoroughly; whisk 2 eggs and stir them into the mixture to make a smooth firm paste. A little milk may be added if necessary. Roll the paste out to the thickness of an inch. Stamp it in rounds, and bake these on tins in a gentle oven. If preferred, ground rice and butter may be used instead of flour and lard. Time to bake, three quarters of an hour.

Cassells Dictionary of Cookery

Norfolk Gingers

4 oz brown sugar; 4 oz butter; 2 teaspoons ground ginger; ½ teaspoon mixed spice; 1 small teaspoon bicarbonate of soda; 8 oz plain flour; About 2 tablespoons milk; 1 egg.

Sift the flour, spices and sugar into a basin and rub in the butter. Dissolve the bicarbonate of soda in warm milk. Add the egg and beat until blended. Stir into the dry ingredients and knead until smooth. Flour the hands lightly, and roll equal-sized small portions of dough into balls. Place well apart on a greased baking sheet. Press each ball lightly on top. Bake at 350°F, 180°C, Gas Mark 4 for 25 minutes. Leave on the baking sheet until they cool.

Fenn Country Apple Cake

1½ lb cooking apples; Juice of ½ lemon; 1 oz of butter; 2 oz castor sugar; 2 rounded tablespoons semolina; 1 oz currants; 3 tablespoons black treacle; 8 oz shortcrust or puff pastry.

Roll out the pastry into two circles and line an eight-inch pie plate with one piece. Peel core and slice the apples. Put apples, lemon juice and butter into a pan, cover and simmer slowly to pulp. Add sugar and semolina, and bring slowly to the boil. Cook gently for 5 minutes or until the mixture has thickened. Remove from the heat and leave until completely cold. Spread half the apple in the pastry case. Sprinkle with currants and put in treacle. Add the remaining apple filling. Moisten the edges of the second piece of pastry and cover the pie. Press edges together well and brush top with a little beaten egg or milk. Bake at 425°F, 220°C, Gas Mark 7 for 30 minutes.

Miss Osman's Seed Biscuits

Two pound & half of dough, half a pound of butter, half a pound of sugar, 3 ozs of Carraway Seeds.

Elizabeth Hicks: late 18th century

Norfolk Ginger Drops

2 oz sugar; 1 tablespoon golden syrup; ½ gills boiling water; 1 egg; 1¼ lb self-raising flour; 1 tablespoon ground ginger; 2 teaspoons ground cinnamon; 2 teaspoons mixed spice; 2 tablespoons weak coffee; ¼ teaspoon ground cloves; 1 teaspoon ground mace; 1 teaspoon bicarbonate of soda..

Whisk egg and sugar in basin till fluffy. Dissolve syrup in boiling water. Add coffee. Stir in egg and sugar. Beat in carefully to all dry ingredients which have been previously sifted together. Have ready a greased baking sheet and drop mixture from a teaspoon on to it, keeping drops about 1½ inches apart. Bake for about ½ hour, 350°F, 180°C, Gas Mark 4.

Cake-in-the-Pan-for-Kate's-Young-Man (Suffolk)

1 lb dough; 4 oz currants; 4 oz sugar; 2 oz lard; 1 teaspoonful spice.

Pull the dough as flat as possible. Put in the lard, and work it well into the dough. Add the currants and sugar sprinkled with the spice, knead well. Divide into four, pull flat again, and place in flat tins. These cakes may be split in half and buttered and jammed, or they may be eaten cold. This is a very old harvest cake.

Mrs Arthur Webb

Sponge Cakes

Fourteen Eggs take out 4 whites, a pound of flour, a pound of sugar. Half a pint of Water the sugar and Water to be boiled together and put to the eggs quite Hot.

Elizabeth Hicks: late 18th century

CHAPTER 6

Preserves, Pickles and Home Remedies

The country housewife had to be self-supporting and it was important to preserve fruit and vegetables for winter use. Jams and jellies were obviously popular to eat with bread, or to use in sweet puddings, but fruit was also preserved by primitive bottling methods in earthenware pots and glass jars, covered with bladders saved from pig-killing (some early recipes even specify a form of sterilisation in a water bath). Later bladders gave way to paper dipped in brandy as a preservative cover.

Vinegar was commonly made at home, either from the 'mash' left after brewing ale, or from fruit, particularly gooseberries. Vinegar pickles were made and a variety of highly-spiced catsups (sauces) which gave zest to cooked dishes, and doubtless helped to conceal the flavour of less-than-fresh meat. Walnuts and mushrooms were particularly widely used, and there is even a recipe for powdered mushrooms for the store-cupboard.

Simple home remedies also had to be prepared at home and were part of the housewife's province, and she always kept a good stock of soothing drinks for sore throats or colds, together with simple ointments for everyday cuts and bruises.

Raspberry Jam

Gather your raspberries in a fine day, pick them from the stalks. Crush them in a bowl with a silver spoon, put to them their weight of Loaf Sugar and half their weight of red currant juice Baked. Boil them half an hour, skim it well the time it boils and put it into pots with brandy papers over them.
Elizabeth Hicks: late 18th century

Suffolk Damson Cheese

Wash damsons well, cover with water and stew. Sieve the flesh and measure the pulp. Allow equal weight of sugar and put into a pan. Stir over low heat until the sugar is dissolved. Bring to the boil and simmer gently until a spoon drawn across the bottom of the pan leaves a clear line. Put into small jars with straight sides (old cups will do) which have been warmed. Cover with waxed discs and then with jam covers when cool. Keep for a year before eating. Turn out to serve with meat, or cut in slices and serve with cream.

Essex Lemon Cheese (1819)

Cream 6 oz butter and add ½ lb of powdered lump sugar. Add 2 oz ground rice, grated peel and juice of 1 lemon and 2 well beaten eggs. Mix well together and put in jars. This recipe came from Burnham-on-Crouch and was a filling for cheesecakes in which it rises and spreads. It is best stored in the refrigerator these days, although it was reputed to keep good 'for several weeks'.

Mrs D.G.'s Apple Jelly

To 1 lb of apples pared and cored add 1 lb sugar powdered and ¼ pint water. Boil it until it is stiff with some strips of lemon peel. It may then be put into a mould and turned out when cold.
Mrs Garden, 1847

Mrs Kent's Mushroom Powders

Wash a Peck of Mushrooms and rub them well with a piece of flannel and cut out all the Worms, put them into a bread pan with 20 cloves and 8 large blades of Mace, and as much beaten pepper as will lay upon a half crown, put in a handful of salt, 3 bay leaves, a little rosemary, 3 onions not very large, and a piece of butter the size of an Egg. Add ½ pint of Vinegar, let all these stew over a gentle Fire till all the liquor is consumed, then put them into an oven after bread is taken out and when they are pretty dry lay them upon a sieve till they are dry enough to powder then bottle them up for use.

Elizabeth Hicks: late 18th century

Mrs Page's Artificial Ass's Milk

Two ounces of Eringo root 2 ounces of stick Liquorice 2 ounces of Pearl Barley 1 ounce of Isinglass ounce of Hartshorn shaving a quarter of an ounce of conserve of Roses boil the above ingredients in 3 pints of water till reduced to a quart when cold it will be a strong Jelly take 2 tablespoonsful with the same quantity of new milk warm at 11 o'clock and at 4 - it is requisite to keep the Jelly in a cool place.

Elizabeth Hicks: late 18th century

Mrs Quelch's White Catsup

Take a pint of white wine vinegar divide it into two parts. Put 9 anchovies into one part and simmer it over the fire till they are dissolved then strain it off and take the other part and put in 9 blades of mace, 9 cloves a little whole pepper, a race of ginger, a nutmeg sliced. Simmer these over the fire a little. When cold mix it with the other half, then put it into a bottle and add a handful of horseradish scraped thin, 4 shalots, a pint of white wine half a pint more vinegar. Shake the bottle full an hour and cork it close. One spoonful is enough for almost any sauce.

Elizabeth Hicks: late 18th century

To Preserve Apricots

Put the weight of sugar to them after they are peeled and the stones taken out put the sugar to them and let them stand all night half an hour will boil them.

Elizabeth Hicks: late 18th century

To Pickle a Mango

Scoop the inside out of a Large Cucumber then fill it with Black Mustard Seed, Ginger, whole pepper, Garlic, Salt & a little Horseradish shred fine, close it up and cover it with good vinegar.

Elizabeth Hicks: late 18th century

Mrs King's Preserves

Cherries, Plums of all sorts, and American apples, gather when ripe, and lay them in small jars that will hold a pound strew over each jar 6 ounces of good loaf sugar pounded, cover with two bladders each, separately tied down, then set the jars into a large stew pan of water up to the neck, and let it boil 3 hours gently.

Elizabeth Hicks: late 18th century

Mr Kent's Damson Cheese

Scald ripe Damsons in as much water as will cover them pulp them through Cullendar whilst they are hot, scald them as they are pulped to 1 pound of pulp, a Quarter of a pound of Sugar, wet it just enough to melt it before it is put to the pulp it must boil a long time, have a quick fire waste about half and let it be constantly stirred or it will burn put it into Moulds.

Elizabeth Hicks: late 18th century

Currant Jam

Half a pint of the Juice of Currants, 3 pounds of sugar set it over the fire till all is dissolved, put in 5 pounds of picked Currants boil and skim it till it is a jelly. Put it in pots set them in the sun a week, tye it down close with Brandy papers over them.

Elizabeth Hicks: late 18th century

Mrs Grove's Way to Pickle White Cabbage

Take a long cabbage, hang it up to drain the wet out for 3 or 4 days, then cut it in small quarters, put it into a jar. Boil as much Vinegar as will cover it, put to every Gallon of Vinegar, 3 ozs of Tamarick, 3 spoonfuls of mace, Mustard, as much salt as you think proper. Boil it all together and put it to the Cabbage hot, let it stand till cold, then put into it a little ginger and tie it down close.
Elizabeth Hicks: late 18th century

To Pickle Mushrooms

Take your Mushrooms wipe them dry and throw them into Milk & Water and then set on your stew pan with half Milk and half Water. When it Boils, put in Mushrooms and let them boil up thick then pour them into a sieve and let them drain till cold. Make your pickle of the best Vinegar & Mace.
Elizabeth Hicks: late 18th century

Mrs Woodgate's Catsup

Take your Walnuts Green, beat them small put them into a pan with a little salt, let them stand all night then strain them through a Cloth, add to juice half red Wine with a Blade of Mace, make it boil and scum it.
Elizabeth Hicks: late 18th century

A Cure for the Jaundice (John Conder Ipswich)

Take 1 oz of red Doc Seed dry, boil it in 3 pints of water till 1 pint is nearly wasted then strain it of and add 3 gill glasses of white Wine. Dose take a gill glass 3 times a day when the stomach is the emptiest, this will be 4 days in taken, then stop 2 days and repeat the Medicine which will with the Blessing of God compleat the Cure be the Jaundice ever so bad.
Elizabeth Hicks: late 18th century

To Preserve Quinces

To every pound of quinces, three qr of a pound of loaf sugar, and Qr pint of water, the pips ty'd in muslin then set them on a slow fire till they look quite red and put them in a jar with brandy paper over them.
Elizabeth Hicks: late 18th century

Miss Houlding's Ginger Lozenges

Half a pound of Loaf Sugar powdered, ¾ ounce of Ginger grated, a small wine glass of water - Boil it till it cands round the spoon stirring well then fine butter a paper and lay in a flat dish and pour it on when a little cool cut it in small square pieces
Elizabeth Hicks: late 18th century

Miss Trap's Pickle

Take three quarters of a pound of Garlic peel and slice it salt it set it by till it draws out the water then pour it off. Put 1 pound of race Ginger into Salt and water let it stand all night then draw it off and cut it in thin slices. Put the Garlick & Ginger into 1 Gallon of Best Vinegar with a quarter of a pound of Bruised Mustard Seed and 2 ozs of long pepper. Just give it a boil if you please. You may add a little Tarmarick to give it a Colour. Put it in a jar close stopped and you put in your things as they come in Season Green Plumbs, Pears, Apples, Carrots, Turnips, Reddishes, Colly Flours, Cabbage Brocoli. Cabbage is best just to boil a little before you put it in, the other things all go in as they come.
Elizabeth Hicks: late 18th century

Revd Mr Bayles' Vinegar

Put on rather more water than you want for 9 gallons on the Mash after you have done Brewing let it stand all night to 9 Galls put 10 lbs of pretty good sugar boil them together about ¾ of an hour. When it is cool enough set it to work with a little yeast the same as you do best after it has done working add 6 lb of Treacle and put into cask let it work a few days and then place it in the sun lay over the Bunghole a piece of Glass or the foot of a wine glass.
Elizabeth Hicks: late 18th century

CHAPTER 7

Wines, Syrups and Cordials

Wine making has always been a favourite country occupation, but it was also a useful way of preserving vegetables, fruit and flowers, and gave a little cheer to dark winter days. Elaborate syrups were often prepared, and cordials which were less alcoholic than wine and often served as a soothing drink at bedtime, particularly for those with colds. Blackberries and elderberries were favourite ingredients, giving a rich colourful wine with a strong flavour. In larger houses, vast quantities of punches and liqueurs were made with cheap brandy and gin.

Suffolk Blackberry Cordial

1 quart ripe blackberries; 1 pint white vinegar; 1 lb loaf sugar; 8 oz honey.
Put the blackberries into an earthenware jar and pour on the vinegar. Leave them to stand for a week, stirring and pressing the blackberries two or three times a day to squeeze out the juices. Strain the liquid into a saucepan and add the sugar and honey, and boil for 5 minutes. Cool completely and pour into dark bottles. Cork well and store in a cool place. Use 1 tablespoon of cordial in a glass of hot water as a good bedtime drink; it is very good for relieving a cold.

Rhubarb Wine (Suffolk)

Measure 1 pint of rhubarb, cut into small pieces, to 1 pint of water, to the quantity you require. Put all together into an earthen vessel and let it stand for a fortnight. Stir and squeeze it (with a wooden spoon) every morning. Then strain off, and measure half a pound of white sugar to every pint of liquid. Let this stand for a week; skim every morning, and bottle at the end of the week.

Mrs Woodgate's Cowslip Wine (Stratford)

Three pounds of blossoms, 4 Gallons of water, 14 pounds of sugar, boil the sugar in the water a little while, when cool work it with a little yeast, the next day turn it to the blossoms into a cask with 3 lemons & with the peels also, stir it with a stick for a few days, then stop it down for 6 weeks, then bottle it with a spoonful of Brandy in each bottle.
Elizabeth Hicks: late 18th century

Essex Blackberry Wine

Put any quantity of blackberries in a pan, just cover them with boiling water, and allow them to stand in a cool oven or outside the cooking-stove all night to draw the juice; or the berries may be mashed with a mallet. Measure and strain into a cask or stone bottle, and allow the juice to ferment for a fortnight. No yeast is required. Then add 1 pound of loaf sugar to every gallon of the wine, with a ¼ pint of best brandy. It may be bottled in 6 months, but will improve by keeping.

Chigwell Hall Claret Cup

6 bottles claret, 2 syphons of soda water, ¼ bottle sherry, 2 lemons sliced thin, 6 tablespoonsful sugar, 2 wine glasses brandy, a little sliced cucumber, sprig of borage.
Lady Savill

Elderberry Wine (Essex)

Remove the berries from the stems and if necessary wash them. Place in a pan, mash well, and pour over boiling water in the proportion of 3 quarts to 4 quarts of berries. Let them remain for 24 hours, then strain and press out all the juice that can be forced through the strainer. For every 2 quarts of juice add 1¾ pounds of loaf sugar, a dozen allspice, an inch of ginger root, and a teaspoonful each of caraway seeds and powdered cinnamon. Boil all together for 5 minutes, and when quite cold, put in half an ounce of compressed yeast, which has been stirred until liquid with a teaspoonful of sugar. The fermentation will commence in a short time, and when it is quite finished the wine may be bottled.

Mrs Kent's Elderberry Wine

Take 16 pounds of Malage Raisins pick and chop them very fine; take 6 pounds of powder sugar and 5 gallons of water; boil them altogether a quarter of an hour, then pour the liquor boiling hot upon the raisins, stir them well together and let them stand 10 days stirring it well every day then strain the liquor and press out the Raisins; add to each gallon a pint of the pure juice of elder-berries. Put to it a very little ale yeast spread upon a piece of toast just enough to make it

move not to work up. Let it stand 2 or 3 days to ferment, then it stand up into a vessel, but let it not be full that they may be room for it to work. Stop it close, let it stand to be thoroughly fine and then bottle it off.
Elizabeth Hicks: late 18th century

Mrs Quilter's Currant Wine (Felixstowe)

Take a Peck of Currants not picked from the stalks. Crush them put four gallons of water. Let them stand 24 hours, then strain them off. To every gallon of liquor put 3 pounds & a half of sugar stir it well together let it stand then take off the scum. Then turn it up and let it 2 months then draw it off and empty the lees, rince the Cask with a little wine, turn it again and put in a pound of Lump Sugar 1 pint and half of Brandy stop it close let it stand till the spring then Bottle it off. Four gallons of water the Liquor when strained 5 gallons. Fill it up till it have done working.

Blackberry Syrup (Essex)

Stew the blackberries with a quarter of a pint of water to every 3 pounds, until the juice is drawn. Strain, and to every pint of juice add 6 ounces of sugar. Boil sugar and juice together for 15 minutes, and bottle for use when cold.

Lemon Syrup (Essex)

Put 12 ounces of loaf sugar into 1 quart of water, and let it boil for 15 minutes, skimming it carefully. Take it off and let it get cold, then add half a pint of strained lemon-juice and 1 drachm of essence of lemon. Mix well and bottle it. Cork very tightly To be used with water or soda-water.

Chigwell Hall Sloe Gin

Pour 1 gallon of gin and 1 gallon of whisky into a 3-gallon jar. Add 8 gallons of sloes which must be well pricked with a needle, 1 oz of bitter almonds blanched and 5 lb of loaf sugar well cut up. Cork the jar well and shake it twice a week for 3 months, Then strain through a jelly bag and bottle and cork well or it will lose colour. Resin the mouths of the bottles.
Lady Savill

Sloe Gin (Essex)

Into 1 quart of best gin put 1½ pints of ripe sloes (some of them bruised) ¾ of a pound of loaf sugar, and ½ ounce of bitter almonds (blanched and well split). Cover the vessel containing the cordial closely, and leave it 6 months, stirring the contents occasionally, then strain off the liquor and bottle for use.

Norfolk Punch No. 1

In 20 quarts of French brandy, put the peels of 30 lemons and 30 oranges, pared so thin that not the least of the white is left; infuse 12 hours. Have ready 30 quarts of cold water that has been boiled; put it to 15 pounds of double-refined sugar; and when well mixed, pour it upon the brandy and peels, adding the juice of the oranges and of 24 lemons; mix well. Then strain through a very fine hair sieve into a very clean barrel that has held spirits, and put 2 quarts of new milk. Stir and then bung it close; let it stand 6 weeks in a warm cellar; bottle the liquor for use, taking great care that the bottles are perfectly clean and dry, and the corks of the best quality and well put in. This liquor will keep many years, and improves by age.

Norfolk Punch No. 2

Pare 6 lemons and 3 Seville oranges, very thin; squeeze the juice into a large jar; put to it 2 quarts of brandy, 1 of white wine, 1 of milk, and 1¼ lb of sugar. Let it be mixed, and then covered for 24 hours. Strain through a jelly-bag, till clear; then bottle it
The Vintner's, Brewer's Spirit Merchant's and Licensed Victualler's Guide 1838

Mrs Nottcutt's Duke of Norfolk

Peel the peels of 12 Seville Oranges and 2 Lemons into 2 gallons of Rum, let them remain there 12 hours, boil 3 gallons of water and when cold put in 6 pound of Loaf Sugar the juice of 14 Oranges and 10 Lemons, mix them altogether; put in a pint of new Milk, let it stand 6 weeks in the cask or till it is quite fine.
Elizabeth Hicks: late 18th century

Mrs Cole's Orange Wine

Boil three quarters of a hundredweight of Loaf Sugar in 28 gallons of Water half an hour skimming it well after which put it in a tub, when nearly cold put in the outward rinds of 6 score Oranges pared very thin, when quite cold put in the juice of 12 score Oranges, let it stand a week stirring it every day, then strain off into the Cask and let the Cask miss an inch of being full, as soon as the wine is turned dip a toasted crust into yeast and put it into the Cask, lay the bung on lightly for 2 or 3 days and stop it down as light as you can. Your wine should not be Bottled till it is a year old. Allow 1 Gallon of Water for waste. This quantity is an exact half Hogshead and is 3 pounds of sugar, and 9 oranges to a gallon of Water.
Elizabeth Hicks: late 18th century

To Make Shrub

Take 8 Seville Oranges and 6 ozs of double refined sugar to a quart of brandy, the orange juice and the sugar together, then strain it through a fine cloth, and mix that and the brandy in a tub, then tun it up into a cask and let it stand 14 days and if it is not fit to bottle in that time fine it down with whites of eggs or isinglass, and when fine put it into bottles.
Elizabeth Hicks: late 18th century

Sugar Beer (Suffolk)

Bring to the boil ½ pint of hops and 1 gallon of water and then simmer for 2 hours. Add honey to sweeten and a tablespoonful of brewer's yeast spread on a toast float. Cover with a cloth and leave overnight. Next day skim off the froth and use. This does not keep more than 2 or 3 days.

Ginger Pop

3 gallons of water, 2 pounds of sugar, 2 ounces of Ginger cut fine, 2 ounces of Cream of Tartar, juice of 2 lemons leaving out one peal. Pour the water boiling hot on to the other ingredients work it with a Yeast Toast when nearly cold. bottle it in 92 hours.

Mrs Hick's Raspberry Vinegar

Put a lb of fine fruit into a China bowl and pour upon it a quart of the best white wine vinegar; next day strain the liquor upon a pound of fresh raspberries and the following day do the same, but do not squeeze the fruit, only drain the liquor as dry as you can from it. The last time pass it through a canvass previously wetted with Vinegar to prevent waste. Put it in a Stone jar with 1 lb of sugar to every pint of juice broken into large lumps; stir it when melted, then put the jar into a pan of water, or on a hot hearth. Let it simmer and skim it and when cold bottle it. This is one of the most useful preparations that can be kept in an house, not only as affording the most refreshing beverage, but being of singular efficacy in complaints of the Chest. A large spoonful or two being put into a tumbler of Water. Be careful to use no glazed or metal vessel for it. The fruit with an equal quantity of sugar makes excellent Raspberry Cakes without boiling.

Elizabeth Hicks: late 18th century

Mrs Colchester's Syrup of Cloves

Clip gilly flowers and take their weight in Sugar, taking a Gallipot and take a layer of flowers and a layer of sugar till the pot is full, put a few spoonfuls of water, tye a cloth over the Top and set it in water over a gentle fire and let it infuse till the strength is out of the flowers which will be in a few hours strain it through a flannel and when cold bottle it up.

Elizabeth Hicks: late 18th century
** This makes use of the strongly scented clove carnations. A gallipot is a stoneware stewpot

CHAPTER 8

Dumplings

Norfolk and Suffolk are the traditional home of dumplings, as the heart of the English cornlands. In the Fens, they are traditionally called 'swimmers', but my village authority tells me that 'Floaters are the traditional Norfolk yeast dumplings which take 20 minutes to cook, while the suet variety are called 'Sinkers'. According to a Norfolk Museum's survey, suet was not used in Norfolk Dumplings. They were made of plain flour and water, or of bread dough using yeast, which could be made at home or bought from the local bakehouse. The dough was shaped into balls (about the size of tennis balls when proved) and boiled for exactly 20 minutes, so they were often called 'Twenty Minute Swimmers', and it was important never to lift the lid from the pan before the time was up, nor to keep a dumpling waiting. Dumplings could be eaten with gravy, or with treacle, or butter and sugar. With gravy, they were often served before the meat like Yorkshire Pudding to lessen hearty appetites. Dumplings should not be touched with a knife, but torn apart with two forks, and any leftover dumpling could be sliced and toasted like bread.

Two other types of dumplings are recorded in East Anglian manuscripts. One is sometimes called a French dumpling and was favoured by Sir Robert Walpole and is filled with dried fruit and spices - it bears a close resemblance to the Scots 'Clootie Dumpling' and possibly has the same origins in France which contributed so much to Scots cookery. The second type of dumpling is a 'drop dumpling' or 'spoon dumpling' consisting of a thick egg and milk batter, spooned into the water and boiled.

Norfolk Dumplings

The farmer's wife very skilfully divided a pound of dough (remember, just ordinary bread dough) into 4 pieces. These she weighed, and so cleverly had she gauged the size that they weighed approximately 4 oz each. She kneaded and rolled them in a very little flour until they were quite round, then put them on a plate and slipped them into a large saucepan containing fast-boiling water. The saucepan lid was put back immediately, and then, when the water came to the boil once more, 15 minutes' rapid boiling was allowed for the dumplings. Gravy was made and four soup-plates were heated in the oven, and as soon as the dumplings had had their allotted time, each was lifted quickly on to a plate, and surrounded with hot gravy; then they were served.

Apparently four things are of importance:

First the dumplings must be of the same size.

Secondly, once in the water, the lid must not be lifted until the cooking is complete.

Thirdly, the pan must be sufficiently large to allow of dumplings swelling to their fullest extent.

Fourthly, they must be dished up on to hot plates with hot gravy and served at once.

Dumplings in Norfolk are not sweet. They are a very substantial part of what might be the meat course, or they serve as a meat substitute. In the villages I found that they were sometimes put into very large pots and boiled on the top of the greens; then they are called 'swimmers'.

Mrs Arthur Webb

Norfolk Dumplings

½ oz yeast; 1 teaspoon castor sugar; ¼ pint hot water; 2 tablespoons milk; 1 lb plain flour.

Cream the yeast and the sugar. Pour the milk and water over the yeast. Put the flour into a basin and pour in the liquid. Mix well and leave to rise in a warm place for 2 hours. Knead the dough well and form into dumplings. Leave them to stand for 10 minutes. Serve hot with melted butter and sugar and eat with two forks. If the sugar is left out of the recipe, these dumplings can be served with gravy.

** *The quickest way to make these dumplings was to take pieces from the bread dough, form into dumplings and cook in the pot.*

Norfolk Dumplings (1765)

Mix a good thick batter as for pancakes with ½ pint of milk, 2 eggs, a little salt and flour. Have ready a clean pan of water boiling, into which drop some of this batter. Be sure that the water boils fast, and boil for 2 or 3 minutes; then throw them into a sieve to drain the water away. Then turn them into a dish and stir a lump of fresh butter into them. Eat them hot and they are very good. These are sometimes called 'drop dumplings' or 'spoon dumplings'.

Norfolk Dumplings (another way)

Take baker's dough and form dumplings the size of a large egg. Then put plenty of sugar, butter and spices into a pan of hot milk, baste the dumplings well with the milk, and bake a golden brown. The dumplings when cooked, should be double the size they were when put into the oven.

Suffolk Dumplings

My mother used to make for my father what he called his Suffolk dumpling - he coming from Suffolk. She used to mix flour with some cold water and shape it into a ball, then put it into a steamer and leave it to stand a while. Then the steamer plus dumpling was put over a pan of boiling water and allowed to cook - to steam. When ready it had blown up ever so much and my father used to pull it apart with two forks and put syrup on it. When my mother and I had it we put gravy from the meat on it. That was between 50-70 years ago. Some years ago I saw a very interesting comment on this recipe, but it was called a Sussex dumpling made from 1 lb of plain flour and ½ pint of cold water, divided into 4 or 8 dumplings. The maker said it was 'light as love' and the secret was to leave the dumplings for several hours in a warm place, then throw them into a pan of fast-boiling water and boil rapidly for 20-45 minutes according to size. They will be as light as a feather because flour and water mixed and left in heat will ferment.

Dorothy Hall, Stockport, Cheshire

Sir Robert Walpole's Dumplings

This recipe was recorded by a Mrs MacIver in 1773. Shred 1 lb of suet small. Grate ¾ lb stale bread. Pick and clean 1 lb of currants. Cut ¼ lb orange peel and citron small. Mix all together and season with cinnamon and sugar. Use 6 or 8 eggs but use only the white of half the number, and all the yolks. Make into a *stiff* paste with the eggs, it must be very stiff indeed. You should have small nets, wrought of small pack-thread; make them all of one size, except one for the middle, make it a little larger. Put them into a pot of boiling water. They will take about one hour's boiling. If you have not nets, you may tie them up in pieces of clean rags, dish them, and pour beat-butter wine and sugar over them.

Hard or Suffolk Dumplings

Put a saltspoonful of salt into a pound of flour, and mix it with as much water as will make it into a stiff paste. Divide the paste into half a dozen balls, dip these in flour, throw them into a pan of fast-boiling water, and let them boil for three-quarters of an hour. Put a little butter in the middle of each ball, or send gravy to table with them. Probable cost 2d. Sufficient for six persons.
Cassells Dictionary of Cookery

Suffolk Pork and Onion Dumpling

This recipe comes from Southwold. Grease a basin. Make a paste with ¾ lb flour, 6 oz suet, ½ small teaspoonful salt and 1½ gills of cold water. Line basin with this, keeping some for the top. Cut 2 lb pork and 1½ lbs of onions in pieces and arranged in alternate layers in the crust, seasoning each with salt and pepper. Add 1 gill water and put crust on top. Tie up and steam 4 or 5 hours.

Suffolk Dumplings

Take 1 pound of dough, divide it into 6 equal parts, mould these into dumplings and drop them into fast boiling water. Boil quickly for 10 to 15 minutes, and serve them the instant they are dished. They should each be slightly torn apart with two forks to let the steam out, directly they are taken out of the saucepan, or they will be sad (heavy) in the middle.

Mrs Crowfort's Dumplings

2 eggs; 8 tablespoons flour; 8 tablespoons milk.

Made into two dumplings and boiled ¾ of an hour. The thick gravy is made by dredging the meat well with flour and adding a little water.

Mrs Garden, 1863

College Dumplings

Two tablespoonfuls each of sugar, breadcrumbs, suet, currants, a good grating of nutmeg, grated rind of ½ lemon, the juice of ½ lemon. Mix all these together in a basin, add a well beaten egg. Form into little cakes and fry for 5-6 minutes. Put on a very hot dish. Sieve a little sugar over. A very nice lunch pudding

Lady Savill

Lowestoft Buttons

Make a batter with flour and milk as required, using just enough milk to give you a good thick mixture. Stir in salt and pepper to taste and beat well. Drop into boiling water a teaspoonful at a time. Cover and boil for 5 minutes. Strain and pile on to a heated platter. Melt a walnut of butter in a small frying pan and add 1 cup fine breadcrumbs. Fry till golden and scatter over the buttons to serve.

Baked Dumplings

Mix 8 oz of plain flour, 2 teaspoons baking powder, 6 oz grated suet and a pinch of salt and mix with milk with a soft dough. Knead into a flat round and put on a greased tray. Mark across the top in a cross with a knife and brush with milk. Bake in a moderate oven (350°F, 180°C, Gas Mark 4) for about 20 minutes until well risen and golden. Serve with a roast or casserole.

Rabbit Dumplings (1859)

Bone a rabbit, cut the meat into shapely morsels: rub them with lemon-juice, white pepper, chopped herbs, and a shred shallot. Wrap each piece of meat in a good pudding crust, carefully fastening them, so as the juice may not escape. Boil them slowly for an hour, and make a sauce with the bones, and small portions of meat. Add the juice of a lemon and serve.

Raisin Roly Poly

Suet had to be minced by hand with a table knife, and raisins stoned likewise. The pudding should be long-shaped and boiled in a cloth, called in Suffolk a 'puddenpoke'. A boy would be told 'you must eat another yard of pudden first' before he could become a man. Long puddings were also eaten with gravy as a softener to the appetite, made with a dumpling mixture.

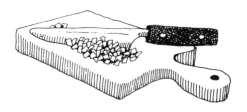

CHAPTER 9

East Anglian Specialities

A few East Anglian goods do not fit into specific food categories, so they have been gathered together in one chapter. Most of these foods were associated with special days, such as the celebration of harvest or sheep-shearing, the important days before Lent, Easter, Christmas and Mothering Sunday. Some food such as Frumenty was made in many other areas, but different versions appeared in East Anglia.

Frumenty

Frumenty or Firmity is a very old dish, occurring in Yorkshire, Staffordshire, Lincolnshire, Suffolk, Leicestershire, Derbyshire, Wiltshire and Hampshire. It was formerly eaten at royal banquets as an accompaniment to savoury meats such as venison and porpoise. It featured at the marriage feast of Henry IV and at the Coronation feast of Henry VII. It was a favourite festive dish, eaten on Christmas Eve with cheese and gingerbread (Yorkshire), Mothering Sunday (Wiltshire) and for a Firmity Tea at sheep-shearing and harvest in Lincolnshire. Bowls of frumenty were sometimes for sale in dairies, or the basic prepared wheat could be obtained, particularly in Wiltshire. In the hunting season in Leicestershire, it was offered by cottages to weary huntsmen. Yorkshire bakers had special days for preparing or 'creeing' the wheat, and the completed dish was sold in the streets of Leicester, Derby and Boston, Lincolnshire. There are many variations on the basic recipe for this kind of fruity porridge, but all depend on the prepared wheat, although sometimes it was made of pearl barley.

Creed Wheat

Wash the wheat and put in a pan or stone jar with a cover. Cover the wheat with cold water 3 times its own measure. Put it in a hot oven early in the day and let it stay as the heat cools until next morning; or put in a pan of hot water on the hob or stove for the same period or longer. The aim is to stew or 'cree' the wheat in water for 24 hours, at the end of that time if the grains are not burst and set in a thick jelly they will be if the contents of the pot are boiled up for 5 minutes.

Plain frumenty consists of this prepared wheat with milk and honey or treacle. The wheat could be boiled up with milk and flavoured with allspice, and then thickened slightly with flour. Raisins nutmeg and cinnamon were additives on special occasions, or a bayleaf or piece of lemon peel could be used. Eggs and cream might be used too. When dried fruit was added, it was considered best to boil the fruit first until 'to the point of bursting'. On special occasions, a little brandy was stirred into the dish.

Suffolk Thruminty or Ferminty

Boil 1 pint of clean wheat in water and, when cooked, leave to cool. Place in a bowl and add 1 lb washed currants, ½ lb chopped suet and 1 lb coarse brown sugar, the juice and grated rind of a lemon and a large apple, peeled and chopped. Mix well and use in pastry to make Harvest Field Pasties.

Suffolk Frumenty

This was eaten during the 12 days of Christmas; some was placed in a plate outside the door at night for the Pharisees (fairies). The Suffolk version of this dish was sweetened with honey and flavoured with cinnamon.

Samphire

This plant is found on the north coast of Norfolk on the edge of tidal waters and marshes, and is eaten during late July and August. Traditionally it was pickled, although it is claimed that rock samphire is better for this purpose. In Norfolk the samphire was heated for pickling in the village baker's oven. To eat fresh, pick from areas where the tide has washed the samphire well. Wash well in fresh water and pick out any weeds. Boil in fresh water for 10 minutes and serve with melted butter. Eat like asparagus, biting off the fleshy parts (it is often known as 'poor man's asparagus').

Pickled Samphire

Do not wash the samphire, but leave the sea salt on it. Put the samphire in a flat bowl, cover with salt and spring water to cover and leave for 24 hours. Put into a clean pan and cover with good vinegar. Set the pan over a very slow fire and let it come slowly to the boil. Take off while the samphire is still green and crisp. Put into pickling jars, pour on the hot vinegar and leave until cold. Seal tightly. Use after a week or two.

Pickled Samphire
(18th century)

Wash your samphire well in sour small beer, then put it into a large preserving pan, dissolve a little bay salt and twice the quantity of common salt in sour beer, then fill up your pan with it, cover it close, and set it over a slow fire till it is of a fine green. Drain it through a sieve, and put it into jars. Boil as much white vinegar as will be sufficient to cover it, with a trace or two of ginger and a few peppercorns. Pour this hot upon your samphires in the jars and tie them down.

Pickled Samphire
(today's way)

We pick it and wash it in fresh water. Then we take off the roots and cook it in water with just an eggcup full of vinegar so the taste of the vinegar cooks in it. Then we put it in Kilner jars with the pickling vinegar. It can be eaten straight away but it lasts right through the winter.

Jack the Painter (Blakeney)

Suffolk-Bang Cheese

There are cases in which dairy farmers skim the milk before they begin to make cheese. These cheeses are remarkable for their hardness, because caseine, independently of the butter, is an exceedingly hard substance; these cheeses are sometimes brought into the market, and they are so hard that they are the subject of many a joke. Of such are the Suffolk-bang cheeses made by frugal housewives in that county, who first take the butter and send it to market, and then make their cheese. It is said of it in derision that 'dogs bark at it, pigs grunt at it, but neither of them can bite it'.

Cassells Dictionary of Cookery

'And so home, where I found my wife vexed at her people for grumbling to eat Suffolk Cheese, which I am also vexed at, and so to bed.'

Samuel Pepys: October 4th 1661

Suffolk cheese was also connected with another saying: 'Hunger will break stone walls, and anything except a Suffolk cheese'.

Kettle Sop (Suffolk)

Sometimes known as 'Civil Sue', this is an old remedy for a sore throat. Crumble bread into a basin and season with salt and pepper and a knob of butter. Pour on boiling water and drink in bed.

Biffins

These dried apples are best prepared in a kitchen range such as an Aga or Esse where a low constant heat can be ensured. Blenheims or Biffins are the only apples (Biffin is a Norfolk derivation of Beaufin) to use, and they used to be prepared in ovens cooling down from the baking of bread and confectionery, and were sold commercially in Norwich. They went into the ovens about 6 p.m. and stayed in all night. A similar confection is prepared in Normandy.

Cottage Biffins

Use red-cheeked apples to dry out slowly, and choose apples which have no blemishes. Put them on clean straw on a wire cake rack. Cover well with more straw. Put into a very low oven for 5 hours. Take them out and press them very gently to flatten them slightly without breaking the skins. Return them to the oven for 1 hour and take them out and press them again. When they are cold, coat them lightly with sugar which has been melted over a low heat without colouring.

Commercial Biffins

Cover an oven tray with wheat straw and put unpeeled apples on the straw. Put on another oven tray weighted with about 10lb. Leave in the cooling oven for 40-48 hours. Serve cold with cream.

Apple Hoglins

Also known as 'Apple Jack', a homely sort of pastry turnover made by folding sliced apples with sugar in a coarse crust and baking them without a pan.

Food for Special Days

In the 18th century, large farms made great quantities of cider in two qualities. At Christmas the best cider was tapped and drunk during all the days during which the yule log, or Christmas block, was burning, which might take 10 or 12 days. The best casks were made 12 months before they were to be drunk. The family and servants took their meals together and during the Christmas season the servants were also allowed the best cider. Accordingly, they kept the worst-burning log until Christmastide so that they could prolong the time when they could enjoy the good cider. A small piece of the log was kept until the next year for the purpose of lighting the new Yule log.

On the morning of Christmas Day, in many large farmhouses, a large quantity of frumenty used to be prepared, and the labourers on the farm with their families, were invited to breakfast upon it. Ale or mead, with a slice of toast and nutmeg floating on it, was kept for Christmas Eve. Hot spiced elderberry wine was the usual tipple for holiday friends.

On Shrove Tuesday, pancakes and coquilles were essential, and on Easter Sunday a tansy pudding. Whitsunday was celebrated with cheese cakes, baked custards and gooseberry pies.

Bury St. Edmunds had its own Simnel Cake, eaten on Mothering Sunday, the fourth Sunday in Lent. God's Kitchel Cake was given to Suffolk children asking the blessing of godparents.

Cry of the Radish Boys

In days gone by, street sellers cried their wares whether these were food, hardware or singing birds. Food cries show something of the variety of food until the end of the nineteenth century:

'Buy my dish of Great Eeles'
Hott baked Wardens Hott' *(stewed pears)*
'Buy a Rabbit, a Rabbit'
Crab, Crab, any Crab'
Lilly White Vinegar'

'Buy any Dutch Biskets'
'Ripe Speregas' (asparagus)
Buy my fat Chickens'
'Buy my Flounders'
'Fair Lemons and Oranges'
'Twelve Pence a Peck, Oysters'

'Four for Six Pence, Mackrell'
'Colly Molly Puffe' *(pastry)*
'Sixpence a pound, Fair Cherryes'
'Delicate Cowcumbers to pickle'
'Any Bakeing Peares'

Among the many cries were those for Samphire, Mussels, Cabbages, Cockles, Hartti Chaks (artichokes), Lettuce, Herrings, Milk, Pippin Pies, Turnips, Rosemary and Bay, Onions, Prunes, Figs, Shrimps, Damsons, Worcestershire Salt, Hot Mutton Pies, Smelts, Periwinkles, Pompcons (pumpkins) and Hot Pudding Pies.

One of the oddest cries was in the form of a ballad called at Great Yarmouth, where about 150 boys were employed to sell radishes each season. The ballad was still in use in 1842:

'Moredosher, Moredosh,**
Come Here, yew-raw,
Spring redosh,
Come two bunch, ee yow-who.
Come you that got money,
Whilst I a' got none
Buy all my spring radishes,
And let me go home.
Come all you pretty maids,
That used to buy any,
For here's your spring radishes,

Two bunches a penny.
Come all yo' old women,
Be joyful and sing,
For here's your old radish boy
Now come agin.
Here I am, Both weary and tired;
For here's my last pennuth,
And I don't care who buy it.'

** *A corruption from 'more radish here' and 'more radish'.*

CHAPTER 10

Elizabeth Ravell's Book

This fascinating book has produced some culinary treasures from East Anglian households and, as they have a distinctive style, it seemed worth grouping them together. For reasons of space, it is not possible to reproduce more than a few of the recipes, and I have chosen those which appear to be key recipes for the period or area, or which are particularly interesting or amusing to read.

The manuscript is written in a number of hands, but the book is clearly labelled as belonging to Elizabeth Ravell in 1704. This in itself is exciting, as it dates the book before the days of wide distribution of cookery books when recipes or receipts were passed around among friends in each neighbourhood, or might occasionally include a recipe from another part of the country if a friend or kinswoman visited.

However, Elizabeth Ravell's book has even greater treasures, for the book had been given to her 'by Mr. Grey after the death of Mrs. Kemp', so that many of the recipes are firmly rooted in the 17th century, and this is indeed proved by some of them which feature Elizabethan sack, froises and florentines. The book begins with many herbal prescriptions from Doctor Wickes and the Lady Vere in a poor hand, and a few prescriptions from Dr Tillotson in an educated hand (although one prescription specifies moss growing on a dead man's skull, and another to be taken at the full moon). There are household recipes for wines, cordials, cakes, biscuits, sweet puddings and homely remedies, and just a few for chicken, turkey, calves head and meat hashes. The book passed through various hands and there is a group of recipes dated 1791. The whole book provides a vivid record of more than one hundred years' cooking in the area around Needham Market and Hadleigh, before recipes were copied from printed books, and while dishes were evolving from the heavily spiced and fruited Elizabethan food into the more practical 19th century country food which we think of as typically regional.

The recipes are printed exactly as written, and a great deal of their charm lies in the eccentric spelling and phrasing.

To Make Sauce for a Pullit or Turkey

Take the yelks of 6 egs half a nutmeg grated 1 handfull of time cut small beat these well then put in a pece of butter put all into the belley of the foull let it rost with it then dissolve 3 anchoves in half a pint of Clarit when the foull is rosted take out the egs and mix with your anchoves and dish it up.

Elizabeth Ravell: 17th century

To Make a Fricacy of Chickings

Take 6 chickings flee them and cut them in every joynt fry them in strong broth half a pint of white wine 2 anchoves 2 shalot sweet margirum and time a little sum large mace then put in a peace of butter 4 yealk of egs a glace of sack a handful of parsly shreed small garnish the dish with lemmons and barburys.

Elizabeth Ravell: 17th century

To Make a Froise

Take 6 egs beat them very well then put in as much fine flower as will make it as thick as batter for biscet Season it with salt an what spice you please then put in a quart of thick creame mix it well then fry it with butter.

Elizabeth Ravell: 17th century
*** A Froise or Fraise was a kind of thick pancake, often made with bacon or apples.*

To Stew Potatoes

Boyle them prety tender then pell them and slice them lay them into a dish put to them one pint of sack the marrow on one Bone a peace of mace lemon pell a few cloves sliced let them stew 2 hours then put into a sauce pan some sweet butter and sugar and sack and when it is melted put in the yelks of 2 egg to thick the sauce then put it into your potats and serve it hot to the table.

Elizabeth Ravell: 17th century
*** This very elaborate treatment of the potato indicates an early recipe when the tuber was still a novelty. It seems excessive to use so much sack (a dry wine popular in Elizabethan times) for cooking them, not to mention the additional sack used in the sauce.*

To Prepare Mussharums

Gather them in a morning after the sun up the best are those which are whit or of a pink color within you may gather from the bigness of a botton to the bigness of a goos egg. Pill the outside of them and take away the honeycombe within but use not them which have black spots or are worm eaten. Wash them in water as you do them then set them on the fire with a little water and boil them a quarter of an hour or till tender boil them softly then take them out of the liquor and lay them on slabs till cold then put them into water and salt till you prepare the pickell for them.

To Pickell Purslain

Take purslain stalks and all boyle them tender in water then dry them in a clorth lay them in gally pots and cover them with vinegar and salt mixt but not so strong as for Cowcumbers, this you must do french beans only gust scold them in the water to green them the vinegar must be salt enough to bare an egg.

Elizabeth Ravell: 17th century
*** This turns into a general pickling recipe half way through. Purslain (or purslane) used to be a popular vegetable rather similar to sorrel in flavour, and can still sometimes be obtained from herb specialists.*

To Preserve the Pickell

Take a little of the liquor they ware boyled in and a little vinegar and white wine nutmeg cloves mace hole pepper 2 or 3 bay leaves quarter the mushrums if large and then boyle them in the pickell a little while and keep them in the pickell close covered the pickell is good to put into hashes in the room of oysters.

Elizabeth Ravell: 17th century

How to Stew Oysters

Take one pint of Great oysters dry them in a clorth then take half a penny lofe and cut it in Round Rises and put between every slice a pease of butter and dowe all the outside very well with butter then tye up in a clane ragg 4

cloves half a nutmeg, peace of mace and lay under the lofe then put in two glasses of sack then lay your oysters and let them simper one hour and half then put the yelk of an egg but not let it boyl after the egg is in but shak it very well together and serve it hot to the table.

Elizabeth Ravell: 17th century

To Make Ginger Breade

Take 2 pound malaseess and so much flower as you may make into a past and put into the flower half a pound of suger 1 ounce of ginger 1 ounce of coriander seed then put in your surrup and half a pint of sack or small beer and work it into a past then work into it 1 pound of butter and make it into what form you will.

Elizabeth Ravell: 17th century

To Make Wiggs

Take half a peck of flower on pint of milk warmed 6 ounces of butter melted in the milk 3 quarters of a pound of sugar 1 pint of ale yest 1 ounce of Carriway Seeds make it into a past and let it ly by the fire a rising then make them into little cakes and bake them a quarter of an hour will bake them.

Elizabeth Ravell: 17th century

The Best Way to Make a Sack Possit

Take a dozen egges exceeding well beaten put them in a pint of sack and stir them well that they curd not: then put to them 3 pints of your best sweet creame half a pound of suger finely beaten and stir them well together till the suger be fully melted strain in together into a bason big enough to receive it all: then set it in the bason on a pot of boyling water keeping boyling until the possit be like a Custord and as thick: then take it off and keep it till you think it be cool enough to eat Strew your beaten spices well and thick upon it and serve it.

Elizabeth Ravell: 17th century

**Another version of this rich dish, similar to Italian zabaglione or French sabayon, needs 30 eggs and strong beer as well as sack, but omits the cream. Yet another version in the book incorporates almonds, must and ambergris.

To Cand Flowers

Take flowers of any sort and pick them make a surrup of sugar and put as many flowers as will go into the surrup boyle them with stiring till they be brused so sugar again then set it to the fire and stir it with the back of a spoon and they will be candid a little suger about them.

Elizabeth Ravell: 17th century

To Make Chiny Ale

Take of Ginger brused 3 ounces cloves on quarter of an ounce nutmegs half an ounce bruse them well then boyl them in 3 pints of ale half an hour with one lemon slised and the peil of an other an 1 pint of sack and when it is almost boyled put in one pound of sugar good and let it boyl a little after the suger is in then put it out and let it stand till it be cold the take 2 gallons of Ale after it is wrought 12 hours put into a pail and set it near the fire and cover it close and beat down the top as it rise and when your other is cold put them together and let them stand 6 hours then put them into bottles into every on put a peace of lemon peal a peace of lofe suger and ty them up and let it stand 12 days before you drink it.

Elizabeth Ravell: 17th century

To Make Coltsfoot Ligziges

Take a pound of Lofe Suger as little water as will wet it let it boyle almost to candy then put to it half a pound of the juce of Coltsfoot then let it boyle till it be very thick then put it to on ounce of the powder of Lickorick on ounce of the powder of annis seeds on ounce of the powder of gomarriback on ounce of the powder of orris let it boil till it be almost suger again then drop them.

Elizabeth Ravell: 17th century

To Make Pagle Wine

Take 6 gallons of water into which put 6 pound of suger when it boyl clarifitt with the whits of 2 or 3 eggs put a peck of cowslops into an eathen pot then put in your water and suger boyling hot of the fire let it stand 24 houres close covered then put in the juice of 2 lemmons and both the peals on pint of sack tost a peace of brown bread and spread it on both sids with yeast put it in cover it close let it stand 24 hours more then strain it and put into your vessell let it stand a fort-night then bottle it up put in a peace of loafe suger, in every bottle.

Elizabeth Ravell: 17th century

**'Paigle' is an East Anglian word for cows-lips. In north-west Essex, where cowslips grow freely, the word is however applied to the rare oxlip, but this is not used for wine-making.

To Make a Hash of any Meat

Take a calves head and boyl it and cut the flesh from the bone in thin small peaves put in a pint of oysters and the liquor season it with pepper and salt large mace and lemon peal put in a ladle full of strong muting broth a bunch of sweet beurbs and 2 cloves 2 shalots the juce of a lemon and let it stew till it be tender then put it into a dish garnished with hors readish and slips of roots and all sorts of flowers.

Elizabeth Ravell: 17th century

To Make a Cock Broth

Take a cock and boyl it a great while then take some raisons of the sun with a bunch of sweet herbs and nutmeg boyl them in the broth then take the yealks of eggs and white wine beat them well together let them boyle a little then put sum suger into it.

Elizabeth Ravell: 17th century

To Make Pork eat like Wesfally

Take a quarter of a young hogg Cut it out like a westfulli then take of niter salt and a double quantity of fine suger mixed with as much ordinary salt as you think will season it rubing it in by the fire have a care you set it not neigh the fire for feare you melt the fat hang it up on the Chimny that it may receive a morderate heat then boyl it when you have occasion

Elizabeth Ravell: 17th century
***Westphalia ham was much prized and early English recipes often suggested a cure for producing a similar result.*

To Make a Veale Florentine

Cut your meat into small peaces season with hearbs on nutmeg 12 cloaves beaton not too small put in one pound of currance on quarter of suger and the yelk of 4 eggs 3 spoonfull of vinerger lay some butter on the tope then lay a puff past on the top of the dish and bake it this you may do of veal that have bin rosted slice in some lemon.

Elizabeth Ravell: 17th century
** *A Florentine was the name for a pie; the use of currants and sugar would have made this version an expensive way of using up cold veal, but in Tudor times a Florentine was a rather special pie served to guests.*

To Make a Carrit Pudding

Take a pint of cream and penny white lofe grated half a pound of suger and half an nutmeg and half as much carrit as bread 2 or 3 spoonfulls of sack and five eggs and half a pound of melted butter mix these together and keep it with stiring after the butter is in will it go in the oven.

Carrit Pudding (2)

Take 2 white love and as much root as bread 2 pints of cream and each a little suger and a little marrow a little ambergrees and a little musk. See if a quarter of an hour will bake it.

Elizabeth Ravell: 17th century
** *Carrots were often used for a sweet pudding. The second recipe sounds a particularly fine one for guests.*

To Make an Almon Puding

Take your Almons when they are blanched as maney as will serve for your dish then put it to 5 yelks of eggs 2 spoonfulls of rose water half a nutmeg a little suger and salt to your tast and marrow cut into it and so set it into your oven but you must butter the bottom of your dish before you put your puding in let not your oven be too hot when it is half baked take the white of on egg and 2 spoonfulls of rose water and fine suger beat them well and do it over with a feather and set it into the oven again then stick it with blanched almonds and serve it up.

Elizabeth Ravell: 17th century
** *This sounds a delicious pudding and the early use of a kind of meringue topping is of particular interest.*

A Resait for Chescakes

Take 3 pints of Creame and great in too meaples biskeet and half a penny lofe then set it over the fire till it boyle then put in 12 eggs well beaten. Stir it over the fire till it be thick then cole it, before it be quit cold put it to a quarter of a pound of butter when cold put in a pound of currance plumpt first in scalding water then put in nutmeg sinnamon and suger.

Elizabeth Ravell: 17th century
** *Naples biscuits were often used as thickening.*

To Make a Good Cake

Take half a peck of flower dried in the oven 3 pounds of butter work it into the flower it will take 3 hours working then take a quart of the ale yeast 2 quarts of creame half a pint of rose water half a pint of sack 16 eggs 8 whites mix these in the flower. Stir them well together. If it be hot by the fire till your oven be hott let it be little hotter than for your cheek when you make ready for your oven put to your cake two pounds of currance 2 pounds of raisons shread so make up your cake put it into your oven stop it close so it will take 3 hours to bake it then take it out. Froth it over with the whit of an egge and rose water strew some fine sugar on the top set it in again that it may ice.

Elizabeth Ravell: 17th century

To Make a Gosbery Custord

You must scold your gosberys then beat them all to peaces leave not a skin hole then put them into your posnet with a peace of butter let them be warm then put your rosewater cream and eggs and sugar let them boyl well together to a quart of goseberys 4 eggs a littel creame a littel peace of butter as much suger and rosewater as you shall think fit.

Elizabeth Ravell: 17th century

To Make Aprecocks Gumbless

Take Aprecocks and coddle them tender then pare them and dry the pulp in a silver plat or bason over coles then set in a store a day or 2 then beat it in a morter with so much sugar as will make it in to a stiff past then colour it with saffron or sanders or chockenell then rowl it in thine long peaces and tye them up in knobs and dry them in a store.

Elizabeth Ravell: 17th century

**Apricots grew in many English gardens, and this is a variation of the popular dried fruit pastes used as sweetmeats, although these were usually prepared in sheets and cut, rather than in little knobs or knots recommended here. Sanders and cochineal were used to colour food with a red tinge.

To Dry Pears or Wordens

Take a small wort and boyl a quarter of honey in it and scum it very cleane and when your wort is very cleane put as many pares as your wort will cover and let them boyl very fast till they be very tender then take them out and put more pears into the wort till it be all drank up when you have drawn bread put your pears into the oven stop it close and in 3 ors time so drying you may keep them all the yeare.

Elizabeth Ravell: 17th century

**Warden pears are small hard cooking pears.

A Trifle Mis Jacobs Way

Take as many Mackeroons as will cover ye Dish. Add as much white wine as will soake them properly. Make some rich boyld custard when cold power it on then some Raspberry Jam Blanched Almonds & Candid Peal. Top it up handsomely with Wip Syllibub. Garnish it or not. Probatum Est.

Elizabeth Ravell: 18th century

** This recipe is in a later hand than others in Elizabeth Ravell's book, and is immediately above another dated 1791 which seems the probable date for the trifle recipe too. It is an interesting transitional recipe from the earlier syllabub made by milking the cow into cider or wine to make a frothing drink. This gradually evolved into a whipped cream and wine confection flavoured with lemon or Seville orange and often with brandy added. The next development was to pour a custard over wine-soaked macaroons and to top it with a favourite syllabub. It is interesting to note in this recipe that the raspberry jam goes on top of the custard, not in the solid bottom layer of the trifle. Candied peel was an unusual addition. It all sounds delicious and 'probatum est' (it has been proved) indicates that it was a well-tried favourite recipe. A far cry from today's concoction of stale sponge cakes and packet custard.